"Struggling to make ends meet in today's economy? You're not alone. In *The Wages of Peace*, Brian Humphreys offers a compassionate yet clear-eyed look at the complex challenges faced by low-income communities, the dangers of flawed theologies in facing these challenges, and a practical road map for a better future. This book is a rallying cry for the church to pursue true shalom by biblically reframing assumptions about wealth and work, by dismantling systemic barriers, and by activating economic equity for all, one living-wage job and empowered voice at a time."

LEONARD SWEET, author, professor, preacher, publisher (The Salish Sea Press), and proprietor (Sanctuary Seaside)

"*The Wages of Peace* serves as an exemplary practical theological guide for Christians deeply concerned with one of the most pressing socioeconomic injustices of our time—pervasive and escalating economic inequality. Humphreys challenges his readers to transition from mere peacekeepers to active peacemakers. He compellingly argues that those committed to the biblical commandments of loving God and their neighbors are naturally called to economic peacemaking. The book's strength lies in its practicality; it provides readers with valuable guidelines for community engagement. These include personal testimonies, problem-solving strategies, and inspirational stories, all presented without casting judgment on any parties or opponents. An essential read for anyone earnestly committed to promoting economic justice and peace in our world."

—ILLSUP AHN, professor of philosophy at North Park Seminary and author of *The Church in the Public: A Politics of Engagement for a Cruel and Indifferent Age*

"So often our doctrines fit into neat and tidy boxes of our own making, but Brian Humphreys demonstrates in *The Wages of Peace* that sometimes the ideas of one category can, and in fact should, interact with others. This practical book offers key insights into how the concept of peace can dramatically influence how we think about economics, poverty, and development. This simple but powerful idea has far-reaching and inspirational implications, and provides not only food for thought but real possibilities and models for how to impact communities."

KEVIN WIEBE, community engagement staff member at Hope Mission, Edmonton, Alberta, and author of *Faithful in Small Things: How to Serve the Needy When You're One of Them*

"In one short book, Brian Humphreys manages the incredible feat of defining and explaining nearly every challenge I have learned in fifteen years of nonprofit work. With indisputable clarity, Humphreys walks readers briskly through the daily economic challenges of millions of Americans. He reorients peacemaking from the usual conversations about war-making into the undeniably practical battleground of daily existence in a capitalist system run amok. Without seeking to find the villain to blame, he firmly (but also gently) lays out an unassailable indictment on the most local warfare we ignore: the third Great War for America is the one we have been inflicting upon each other with unrelenting violence. And we are culpable.

"*The Wages of Peace* lays out the problems, connects to common (mis)conceptions about what Scripture says, and invites us to active, solution-focused conversation. Using a format that invites the reader to truth but outlines how readers can discuss solutions, Humphreys lays out a process for changing our conversations together."

KEVIN RESSLER, president and CEO of the Alliance for Health Equity and former president and CEO of the United Way of Lancaster County, Pennsylvania

THE

WAGES

OF

PEACE

THE WAGES
OF PEACE

*How to Confront Economic Inequality
and Love Your Neighbor Well*

BRIAN HUMPHREYS

Harrisonburg, Virginia

Herald Press
PO Box 866, Harrisonburg, Virginia 22803
www.HeraldPress.com

Library of Congress Cataloging-in-Publication Data
Names: Humphreys, Brian (College teacher), author.
Title: The wages of peace : how to confront economic inequality and love
    your neighbor well / Brian Humphreys.
Description: Harrisonburg, Virginia : Herald Press, [2024] | Includes
    bibliographical references.
Identifiers: LCCN 2024019169 (print) | LCCN 2024019170 (ebook) | ISBN
    9781513813769 (paperback) | ISBN 9781513813776 (hardcover) | ISBN
    9781513813783 (ebook)
Subjects: LCSH: Economics--Religious aspects--Christianity. |
    Poor--Religious aspects--Christianity. | Income distribution--Religious
    aspects--Christianity. | Equality--Religious aspects--Christianity. |
    BISAC: RELIGION / Christian Living / Social Issues | BUSINESS &
    ECONOMICS / Development / Economic Development
Classification: LCC BR115.E3 H83 2024 (print) | LCC BR115.E3 (ebook) |
    DDC 261.8--dc23/eng/20240618
LC record available at https://lccn.loc.gov/2024019169
LC ebook record available at https://lccn.loc.gov/2024019170

Study guides are available for many Herald Press titles at www.HeraldPress.com.

THE WAGES OF PEACE
© 2024 by Herald Press, Harrisonburg, Virginia 22803. 800-245-7894. All rights reserved.
Library of Congress Control Number: 2024019169
International Standard Book Number: 978-1-5138-1376-9 (paperback);
    978-1-5138-1377-6 (hardcover); 978-1-5138-1378-3 (ebook)
Printed in United States of America
Cover references: Valeriia Dorofeieva / iStock / Getty Images Plus;
    ardasavasciogullari / iStock / Getty Images Plus

28 27 26 25 24   10 9 8 7 6 5 4 3 2 1

CONTENTS

Foreword 9

Introduction 13

1 Blessed Peacemakers............................ 19

2 Devoured Houses................................ 47

3 The Golden C̶a̶l̶f̶ Bull 73

4 The Planks in Our Eyes 107

5 Local Economic Peacemaking 131

6 Complementary Peacemaking Strategies........... 161

7 Policies for Peacemaking 183

8 Resilient Peacemakers 207

9 Greater Things 237

Notes... 247

The Author.................................... 253

This book was written on the traditional homelands of the Puyallup Tribe. The Puyallup people have lived on and stewarded these lands since the beginning of time and continue to do so today. I pray that this land acknowledgment and hopefully this book itself are small steps toward making true peace. In all endeavors, peacemakers commit to uplifting the voices, experiences, and histories of the Indigenous people of this land and beyond.

FOREWORD

A tent from Resurrection City during the 1968 Poor People's Campaign was painted with a passage from the Hebrew Bible in Genesis 37:19–20: "And they said one to another, behold, this dreamer cometh. Come now therefore, and let us slay him, and cast him into some pit, and we will say, some evil beast hath devoured him: and we shall see what will become of his dreams. MLK Jr. 1929–1968."

In what would be the last campaign that he waged before being assassinated, the Rev. Dr. Martin Luther King Jr. proposed uniting and organizing thousands of poor people from all over the country into a force to be reckoned with. He suggested that the "Achilles' heel" of racism, poverty, and militarism in these yet-to-be United States was to unite millions of poor people across race, geography, and concern into a Poor People's Campaign to lift the load of poverty. Rev. Dr. King proclaimed that the Vietnam War had turned the War on Poverty into a skirmish, and it would take drawing poor people together to stop such a cruel manipulation of those in poverty.

Rev. Dr. King was killed as he pursued this Poor People's Campaign. When he was assassinated, much of the power and organizing of such a campaign of the poor—the dream of decent wages, housing, and social programs—was assassinated alongside him. Demonstrating this feeling, a banner on the Mule Train to Resurrection City that left Marks, Mississippi, the poorest town in the nation, just weeks after Rev. Dr. King's assassination read, "I had a dream." Another read, "Don't laugh, folks, Jesus was a poor man."

In the roughly fifty years since Rev. Dr. King's death, poverty has increased by 60 percent—and there has been continued virtual silence on the issues. All these years later, the world is on the brink of nuclear war, wages are historically low, climate change is wreaking havoc on the poor first and worst while inequality only widens and the costs of living rise. Indeed, Rev. Dr. King's call to address the tripartite evils of systemic racism, economic exploitation, and war is more timely than ever.

In today's political and economic landscape, the United States budgets hundreds of billions for the Pentagon and war but cuts education, healthcare, and other programs of uplift for the poor. Echoing the Bible passage "For where your treasure is, there your heart will be also" (Matthew 6:21), it is clear the value that US society places on militarism and war over healthcare and education for the poor. Far from being intractable, however, ending poverty is possible. If we raised the federal minimum wage to a living wage, communities, especially poor and low-income ones, would experience a ripple effect as that money is circulated back through the economy faster and further than the billions Congress gives the rich and corporations through tax cuts.

We could gain close to a trillion dollars annually in estimated revenue from fair taxes on the wealthy, corporations, and Wall Street.[1] We could invest in public infrastructure and create more jobs outside of the military that could speed a clean energy transition, which would be good for our country and the planet. We could provide healthcare, housing, and education for everyone in this country. After all, feeding people is not only better for the economy than military spending—it creates a more just and peaceful society.

In the richest country in the world, we have abundant resources. The problem is our public policies have funneled too much to too few. And as that banner on the Mule Train reminds us still today, for anyone who claims to be a Christian, the Jesus whom people follow was an unhoused, low-wage worker, born to a migrant, teenage, unwed mother, who traveled around the countryside setting up free healthcare clinics. He was anointed to bring the good news of justice—rather than the bad news of eviction, criminalization, and low-wages—to the poor.

God does not ordain poverty. The poor will be with us only as long as we are disobedient to God. Poverty is the creation of people—of our immoral budgets and unjust policies—and we can choose to end it. In fact, the book of Deuteronomy says that when you forgive debts, increase programs that lift up the poor, pay your workers a living wage, release those who are oppressed, and lend out money knowing you may not get paid back, your whole society will flourish.

We need a moral revolution of values that places the needs and demands of the poor and the planet at the heart of our budget, at the center of our national discourse, at the core of our structures and policies. This will create more jobs, build up our infrastructure, strengthen our economy, and protect our resources for future generations. This will redound to the benefit of all, instead of the few.

This is the importance, and the main idea, of this book. It shows that peace is possible. It is, in fact, far less costly than violence and war—in both lives saved through conflict resolution and negotiation and in economic benefits—to lift from the bottom so everybody rises. Let us heed the words of Brian Humphreys and wage peace. May it be so.

—Liz Theoharis
Ttheologian, pastor, author, executive
director of the Kairos Center, and
co-chair of the Poor People's Campaign

INTRODUCTION

Years ago, I facilitated a monthly community meeting with stakeholders and residents from the city where I worked. We reviewed data about housing affordability and living wage jobs in the area, trying to figure out the right balance of workforce development to help households afford whatever housing might be available and long-term strategies to increase housing density and bring down the cost of renting and buying. This was a historically blue-collar region with many manufacturing and warehouse jobs. Not only were these jobs changing due to new technologies, offshoring, and consolidation, but the wages could not keep up with the buying power of white-collar workers moving in from the metropolitan area north of us.

It was a good meeting—we had honest conversations about the data and our limited knowledge of solving these complex problems—but it was somewhat underwhelming because real solutions evaded us. Wages were close to what they had been a decade earlier, though the cost of living had increased dramatically. Some jobs paid a living wage—roughly speaking, the minimum income necessary to meet a person's basic needs—but many required four-year degrees that could not be attained in the area, which meant those jobs were being filled by workers from other communities, compounding the problem.

Fortunately, the wages of historically blue-collar jobs were rising, and we had several community and technical colleges. But more work needed to be done to understand employers' demand for the degrees those training providers offered. There was a disconnect with the employers claiming that people coming out of those colleges needed to have the proper training or experience to hire. Did we need to emphasize paid apprenticeships to fill the gap, or did we need to help those employers have more realistic expectations for how much experience the next generation of workers have, and support employers to equip new hires with specific skills or techniques? We were getting closer, but every step of the way was more challenging than we thought it should be.

While we struggled with this aspect of the work, other indicators in the community were alarming. The high school representatives in the community group often talked about youth mental health. Demand at the food banks was increasing, and more households were using them for the first time. Eviction rates and certain types of crime were increasing, such as property and car theft. Tent encampments were becoming more visible and frequent, prompting more phone calls to local elected officials and the police department. We knew that with increased homelessness comes increased substance use disorders, complicating strategies such as workforce development training. We also knew we were transitioning from retraining a workforce for a changing economy to supporting households from falling through the cracks, which would make the path to thriving with a living wage job even more complicated and expensive.

After the meeting, people stayed to chat and catch up with one another. I introduced myself to three new people and listened for a while. They expressed frustration at a transitional housing project in their city just a few miles east of us. Seven years earlier, a group in another state had invested in a transitional housing complex in their city. It had twenty-one units converted from rundown apartments into nicely updated transitional housing. (Transitional housing operates as a short-term support while someone figures out longer-term housing options.) These units were not overly fancy but were clean, new, and affordable. The out-of-state investors did not pay close attention to the project because they were so far away, so they hired a management company that stipulated that the households would only pay 30 percent of their income, whatever it was, in rent. They hoped this would allow the households time to get their lives in order and then move out, maybe even purchasing their own homes, and then those units could be backfilled with new households needing longer-term transition, who could then also get back on their feet, and so on.

However, this management company and the group that established the transitional housing made one error. They did not establish definitions for what thriving or "getting back on their feet" meant. There was no specification for when a household was ready to move on and vacate a unit. The coordinators assumed that these households would elect to do so when they were ready. They offered long-term leases to twenty-one households below the federal poverty line—an income bracket that is relatively limited in western Washington. Even a part-time job working the state minimum wage (currently $15.74 an hour) can put a household over the federal poverty line (currently $15,000 to $30,000 depending on household size). So these households were among the poorest of the poor.

They were in dire straits when they moved into the transitional housing units.

Seven years later, those twenty-one households were still there. Those in the coordinating organizations had conversations about finally evicting the households because they had all stayed far too long, and members in each of those households had good jobs now and should be able to move out on their own without any problems. These three people at the community meeting were discussing what the timeline would look like and what changes would need to be made to the new leases when different households were brought in.

Their conversation about these households was light-hearted, more gossip than a serious discussion. But I was curious. I affirmed the frustration that these thriving households hadn't moved out yet. Still, were all twenty-one households really financially stable enough to live independently? They confirmed this was the case.

We paused to consider the implications. It seemed they had stumbled upon a solution to poverty: provide families with supported transitional housing for a sufficient period, and they generally prosper. Initially, these families had focused on recovering from the stresses of poverty. As they healed, they secured entry-level jobs, and with stable housing, their work performance improved. Over time, they advanced to better positions or entered training programs in fields like HVAC, construction, or network administration, eventually earning more than the management company's staff.

The problem, of course, is that it would take more work to scale this solution. How much would it cost to provide five or seven years of supportive transitional housing so households could rest, heal, regroup, and prepare to thrive in this complex, expensive, globalized, rapidly evolving economy? Then again, how much does it cost *not* to do this? What is the cost of three to six months of supportive housing with some résumé writing and job interview practice that we know does not lead to permanent solutions? And how does this failure to meet the needs with sufficient generosity and empathy affect the peace and our ability to be effective peacemakers worldwide?

I have worked in community economic development in various roles, domestically and internationally, for twenty years. I have raised a lot of money, managed many projects with community leaders and organizations, and built various experimental initiatives to address complex challenges and systems. Whenever I encounter such a profound challenge, question, or obstacle, I look over my shoulder, expecting the proverbial cavalry. The Calvary cavalry. The solution could be clearer, but we know the direction to go. We know the work will be more frustrating and require more generosity and grace than we should reasonably expect.

That is what I call a Jesus-shaped hole in the world. This is an opportunity to show up as Christians in the way Christ showed up for us. We didn't deserve any help, and the help we got was far more than we should have expected. And even when we continually reject and take that help for granted because of our selfishness and alternative desires, that grace remains, waiting for us to repent and do better.

In many ways, good and faithful servants are responding. In churches, neighborhoods, and individual relationships around the world, Christians give, respond, and empower. But many of us need to figure out where to start if we want to address these complex socioeconomic challenges. Others of us have hit walls in the work we are currently doing and need to think about living wage jobs or policies that we have not considered before. And some of us mounted up only to ride in the wrong direction to defend an idol we mistook for a divine calling.

In a complex world, we can get distracted by simple narratives. Money, the economy, and poverty are especially susceptible to simplistic storytelling. When it feels like the world is changing too fast, we can be tempted to fashion idols that might provide the stability we seek. When Christianity seems to be in decline, it can be tempting to seize power to maintain dominance.

But what a fantastic time to stop and wonder: What is God doing in the world? How do we hear and obey the calling to participate in the story God is telling and to love the small acts of service and faith that add up to a big effect when all the believers do so simultaneously?

There has never been a better time to be a peacemaker and to love our neighbors as ourselves, according to what they tell us they need, rather than what we want to give them. The only caveat is that much of the time, our neighbors will tell us that what they really need is a job.

DISCUSSION QUESTIONS

1. Do the complexities this group was talking about, such as housing, jobs, and homelessness, mirror concerns in your community?
2. Are collaborative meetings like this one taking place in your community?
3. Are there stories you tell in passing, or could tell, that might resonate with someone unexpectedly?

1

BLESSED PEACEMAKERS

Throw a little love their way . . . and you'll bring out their best!
—The Trolls, in *Frozen*

Nothing stops a bullet like a job.
—Father Gregory Boyle

Several years ago, I convened a beer-and-hot-wings meeting for some men in my city of Tacoma, Washington. I had been working in the early childhood development sector for some time and was surprised by how few fathers were taking advantage of the available resources. These men and I talked about how fathers in our city struggled. They needed resources and encouragement but did not know where to find them and did not trust that the resources they might find would lead to a different outcome. Everyone at that meeting, all of whom happened to be fathers themselves, got excited about doing something about this, and it morphed into an initiative to build community among at-risk fathers and offer them services in a high-trust, culturally sensitive environment.

One of the dads in this group likes to remind us about the temptation to sell drugs in our city. People like me who are White and middle-class often underestimate how little the threat of being arrested deters such behavior, because many people who sell drugs have already been in jail. Often they have already encountered law enforcement for less deserving reasons. As Michelle Alexander describes in *The New Jim Crow*, "The stark and sobering reality is that, for reasons largely unrelated to actual crime trends, the American penal system has emerged as a system of social control unparalleled in world history."[1] The US justice system targets people of color, especially Black men, relegating millions to second-class status. As such, many men of color from our group, like this dad, count jail as a cost of life. That is, until they become parents. They want to be available for their kids and to set a good example. But then things in this economy get hard. Without sufficient income, they are tempted. They likely work low-wage jobs that barely pay enough to cover rent while they see their peers flouting the law and driving new luxury SUVs.

At the beginning of the COVID-19 pandemic, that dad on our leadership team lost his warehouse job as businesses shut down. He was ineligible for unemployment assistance because of a custody issue. He found another job a few months later, but he often talked about the temptation to return to selling drugs out of desperation. Fortunately, he avoided that temptation with our network's assistance and support. But it illustrated the more complex and nuanced obstacles to pursuing peace through economic intervention. If a job that paid $25 or $30 an hour had been readily available, he would have quickly accepted it, and there would have been no question about selling drugs as a viable alternative.

Later, he was connected to an employer who trained him to earn a Class A commercial driver's license. Not only did he do better financially after that, but his personality, confidence, and enthusiasm to model himself as an example to his kids grew. The shame of not being able to provide for his kids was gone. He talked about how eager he was for his son to follow his example and learn these skills to get a good-paying job that offered him a dignified life much earlier in adulthood. Still, the trucking sector has a notoriously high turnover rate.[2] The industry often promises high pay, but earning sufficient income requires many days away from home, and often many additional expenses reduce drivers' take-home pay. This dad struggled to make this job work, and when his family suffered a medical emergency, he had to quit.

This is just one manifestation of a problem in many of our communities. There are symptoms we know to look for, such as crime rates, drug usage, jobless rates, and evictions. And there are symptoms behind closed doors, such as abuse, depression, hunger, sickness, and anxiety. These problems have always existed and will continue to exist to some degree, regardless of what we do. As even Jesus acknowledged, the poor will always be with us.

But the scope and scale of symptoms have become too much to shrug off. Each time some servant-hearted individual gets tired of seeing the same problem in so many individuals and families and starts to follow the breadcrumbs to the source, they seem to reach a similar conclusion: Even in the world's wealthiest nation, it is too hard to earn enough money to thrive without a tremendous advantage of privilege or luck. Wages are far too low and the cost of living is too high. The gap is widening, we are struggling to help communities adapt, and the situation is being exploited by people who make money or attain power through fear and outrage. This will lead to outcomes no one wants.

For Christians, this seems to be the perfect place for the church to intervene and respond to the call to be peacemakers. The world needs radical empathy, service, and generosity. That is the language of Christians, but we struggle to know how to proceed in this complex, globalized world. My hope is that this book will equip more of us to engage with productive empathy as we work to love our neighbors by building more thriving, sustainable, peaceful communities.

In these pages, I focus predominantly on the US context, where I've done most of my work in the past few decades. But my perspective is also informed by work in international contexts, including serving in the Dominican Republic as a Peace Corps volunteer. As we'll explore, economic peacemaking depends heavily on context and community—the specific needs of specific people and places. No matter where you seek to make peace, I believe that the themes and ideas in this book can inform economic peacemaking in any community.

MAKING PEACE WITH MONEY

Economic peacemaking does not mean displacing other ministries or programs. Emphasizing living wage jobs complements and enhances our efforts. Whether we work in mental health, youth development, early childhood education, affordable housing, or other social services, at some point a living wage job is the primary outcome we are looking for, or it is necessary to sustain other outcomes we hope to achieve. In early childhood development, we discuss protective factors to ensure the health and well-being of children and families. One of those factors is concrete support for parents or ensuring parents can afford basic needs such as housing, food, and diapers. A parent who is fatigued and anxious from trying to reliably meet these needs may struggle to engage with other important caregiving factors, such as the social-emotional development of children or nurturing and attachment.[3]

After the housing bubble burst in the mid-2000s and sparked the Great Recession, there was considerable gun violence among youth in my community. In 2011, a teenage boy was shot and killed. His mother became an advocate for more productive activities for youth in the community. She convinced the city and the state to fund a new community center, which opened in 2018. Like many other communities, we have recently seen further increases in gun violence, especially among and affecting youth. We are again asking what interventions are required to make a more sustainable peace.

Ironically, some conversations happen in the center constructed to make peace the last time. The idea was sound, but the execution proved to be complicated. It can be frustrating to work with at-risk youth, and there are few income-generation opportunities. The programs available to low-income youth at the center gradually became more expensive because fewer people used them. Resources were increasingly restricted, with hours reduced. Following through on this peacemaking work would require a longer-term financial and programmatic commitment.

In 2013, I was invited to manage a cross-sector collaborative initiative without a clear purpose or direction. Still, everyone in the room obviously wanted an economic outcome. Representatives from the K–12 system, higher education, nonprofits, and community groups all attended, along with economic development professionals. More people needed better-paying jobs. We needed more information from economic development professionals, employers, and higher education. We needed actionable data about real jobs that pay a living wage and the skills required to get hired. At that time, people were still discerning how bad the housing affordability issues would become over the next decade. Still, we knew the housing market would increase as we emerged from the Great Recession and that interest rates would eventually go up.

The economic development sector also needed to be equipped to participate in this kind of partnership. To their credit, they were doing what economic development boards (commonly established by regional governments) are expected to do: promote economic growth and overall economic well-being. EDBs celebrate business and offer tax incentives to bring in other businesses, but they need to become more accustomed to working with stakeholders from low-income communities. EDBs have essential resources, connections, and information about local economic opportunities, but that information rarely trickles down to the households that need it most. Without proactive relationship-building, low-income communities can get left behind as the job opportunities change, in part thanks to the EDBs. Many traditional economic development practices lead to job growth for an outside workforce with the required skills, which raises the cost of living for the existing households, trained for jobs that might be in decline. Eventually, this can lead to displacement as the community becomes less affordable. Economic peacemaking brings together the two ends of the spectrum: the businesses that offer living wage jobs and the workforce that needs preparation in order to compete for those jobs.

For several years, I experimented with and developed pilot initiatives. The work primarily involved communication to help people in the community understand specific information about job opportunities and provide wraparound services to help them attain the competencies or certifications required for those jobs. The information we currently give people is quite generic. "Go get an education," we often say, but they've seen their peers go to community college, come out with a two-year business degree, and work an entry-level job in an office for $1 more per hour than at a local fast-food restaurant. People need specific information about a particular job, the employer, the employer's wages, and precisely what that employer is looking for in a prospective employee. This is language and context that few people know how to provide.[4] However, building relationships and making connections tends to be a natural skill set for Christian communities and anyone committed to making peace.

Financial worries are growing for many of us. In developing economies, the line between being low-income and middle-class is fading, and not for the better. I hear folk stories about a time when you could get a good job with any college degree, or how even a high school diploma or GED could get you a job in your local community that paid enough to meet your basic needs. If you had smarts or some work ethic, you would thrive. If you were lazy, you would be in a rundown apartment somewhere with a dead-end job. (These stories rarely account for inequities faced by people of color, women, and people with disabilities.)

Today, if you are clever, hard-working, and well-educated, then with some luck or family wealth you might attain a middle-class lifestyle. If you are anything less than that, you are increasingly at risk of extreme poverty or homelessness. Wages are low and the cost of living is very high. Good-paying jobs attract hundreds if not thousands of applications. Sometimes I imagine the California Gold Rush of 1849, when people headed west in a desperate search for treasure. Now, we have a Jobs Rush, and most people find themselves going from job application to job application only to find someone else has gotten there first.

Much has been written about the evolving perception of the Simpsons. Yes, *The Simpsons* Simpsons. When the show first aired in the late eighties, it was about a lower-middle-class family in a rundown home, always jealous of the higher quality of life of the Flanders family next door. Homer Simpson is famously lazy but manages to hold on to a job nonetheless. Viewers watching the show today see the same context but perceive something aspirational and unattainable. The Simpsons have a mortgage they can afford on a large house, a car, food on the table for three kids, and a single income-earner who does not have a college degree. What was once considered a low-income household would now require above-average wealth to attain. Yes, it is a cartoon, but one that helps illustrate how much the economy has changed in the last few decades and how hard it is to not fail, let alone achieve any life goals.

Christian servants aspiring to be peacemakers in the world need to be equipped to talk about money, work, and economic systems. We then find ourselves simultaneously empowering people in low-income communities to survive our complex economy and advocating for this economy to work more equitably for more people.

This is neither easy nor popular. Making peace in the world offends people in and out of the church who either benefit from our current economic system or believe overly simplistic narratives about why so many people are struggling.

Economics and peacemaking may seem odd bedfellows. When we talk about peacemaking, it is often relational and overlaps with spiritual outcomes in the community or even evangelism. Economics reminds us of money, and the Bible is clear about the dangers of money. And yet we are experiencing a lack of peace largely because of the lack of an economic framework from the church—a theology of economics, if you will. Without such a framework, we are left vulnerable to defaulting to the world's philosophy of money and wealth.

Like it or not, we live in a world dictated by money. And not just money, which has always been around and a major driver of behavior. We live in a world of finance, with its globalized stock markets and central banks. And within these complex systems, inequity and discrimination abound. The United States, for example, has a complicated history of denying Black and Brown individuals and communities equal economic participation. We used economics to disturb the peace, and in the name of Jesus, we should be reconciling and pursuing peace through an economic lens.

CHRISTIAN PEACEMAKING

Talking about peace and peacemaking as a Christian can be surprisingly complex. For those of us engaged in the work of loving our neighbors, it can seem intuitive. If someone asks us what it means to be a Christian peacemaker, many will say, "Just look at my life. Hopefully, that's a good example." But if we are pressed to discuss what the Bible says about making peace, we encounter some of the more challenging parts of Scripture to reconcile.

On the one hand, talk about peace appears throughout the Bible:

- The prophet Isaiah anticipates the coming of a "Prince of Peace" (Isaiah 9:6) and declares that "the fruit of. . . righteousness will be peace" (32:17).
- Jeremiah 29:7 counsels, "Seek the peace. . . of the city"—a line that can be found posted on the walls or marketing materials of many Christian nonprofit organizations.

- The wise King Solomon declares, "Deceit is in the hearts of those who plot evil, but those who promote peace have joy" (Proverbs 12:20).
- King David is clear and brief, telling us, "Turn from evil and do good; seek peace and pursue it" (Psalm 34:14) and "Love and faithfulness meet together; righteousness and peace kiss each other" (85:10).
- Jesus says "Blessed are the peacemakers" as part of the Beatitudes (Matthew 5:9).
- Paul talks about peace a lot, including this sampling: "If it is possible, as far as it depends on you, live at peace with everyone" (Romans 12:18); "The kingdom of God is not eating and drinking, but righteousness and peace and joy in the Holy Spirit" (14:17 NKJV); "Let us therefore follow after the things which make for peace" (14:19 KJV); "God has called us to peace" (1 Corinthians 7:15 AMP); and "Be at peace among yourselves" (1 Thessalonians 5:13 ESV).
- Peace is one of the fruits of the Spirit (Galatians 5:22).
- Servants of the Lord "must not participate in quarrels, but must be kind to everyone [even-tempered, preserving peace . . .]" (2 Timothy 2:24 AMP).
- The "wisdom from above" is pure and peace-loving (James 3:17 ESV).
- In a text commonly attributed to the sword-wielding apostle Peter, we are told to "turn from evil and do good; . . . seek peace and pursue it" (1 Peter 3:11).
- Not to mention that the many variations of "Grace and peace to you!" would make for a dangerous drinking game.

The theme of peace also intersects with themes of money and wealth in the Bible. (In fact, Scripture talks about money at least as much as it talks about peace.) "Those who consider themselves religious and yet do not keep a tight rein on their tongues deceive themselves, and their religion is worthless," James writes in a passage that is deeply relevant to our lives today. "Religion that God our Father accepts as pure and faultless is this: to look after orphans and widows in their distress and to keep oneself from being polluted by the world" (James 1:26–27).

The actions of the early Christians right after Pentecost, when the Holy Spirit comes down, seem especially instructive. In Acts 2, on the day of Pentecost, the Holy Spirit filled each of the apostles, and then Peter stood up and preached to the crowd. The people were "cut to the heart" (v. 37), and about three thousand were baptized. After that,

> They devoted themselves to the apostles' teaching and to fellowship, to the breaking of bread and to prayer. Everyone was filled with awe at the many wonders and signs performed by the apostles. All the believers were together and had everything in common. They sold property and possessions to give to anyone who had need. Every day they continued to meet together in the temple courts. They broke bread in their homes and ate together with glad and sincere hearts, praising God and enjoying the favor of all the people. And the Lord added to their number daily those who were being saved. (vv. 42–47)

Teaching, fellowship, wonders, and signs are immediately followed by selling property, giving to anyone with needs, and continually coming together and breaking bread with each other with glad and sincere hearts. Today, there seems to be a lot of hope and anticipation for more such revivals, and that's great. I pray for a revival of action. The modern equivalent of those acts will include joyfully providing economic opportunities for our neighbors and communities.

So, for Christians, peace is a whole thing. Making peace, seeking peace, keeping the peace, being at peace. The counter-arguments to Christian peacemaking range from bad faith to missing the point to genuinely thought-provoking. Christians should let themselves prayerfully ponder and research the role of violence in the Bible and theology. How is the God of the great flood, who sent an angel to kill all the Egyptian firstborn children for Passover, who slaughtered the Canaanites to create the promised land for the Israelites, who seemingly killed Ananias and Sapphira for lying about how much wealth they were giving to the members of early church, the same God who tells us to make peace?

Honestly, I struggle with that question myself. But for those who seek to be Christian peacemakers, the most frequently cited challenge is Jesus' words in Matthew 10 when he quotes the prophet Micah: "Don't think that I have come to bring peace to the earth. I did not come to bring peace, but a sword. I have come to make this happen: 'A son will be against his father, a daughter will be against her mother, a daughter-in-law will be against her mother-in-law. A person's enemies will be members of his own family'" (vv. 34–36 ICB). We intuit that using Jesus' words to justify any behavior that leads to divisiveness is a misinterpretation, but we might struggle to articulate how.

I teach graduate students in Christian community development programs. My students frequently lament that they expected the secular world to push back against their innovative approaches to ministry to love their neighbors better and for the faith community to have their backs. However, most of the antagonism they experience is from their church communities. A student discovered that LGBTQIA+ individuals are significantly overrepresented among the people experiencing homelessness in her community. This student assumed that the church she grew up in would be enthusiastic to love these neighbors even if they disagreed with the cultural issues around gender and identity. But many people in the church rejected this conclusion and said hurtful things to and about her. She came away from that experience deconstructing her faith and struggling with what it means to be a Christian.

I believe that this intimate betrayal is what Jesus was talking about. Following Jesus is not a clear, straight line. It requires dying to ourselves daily and taking up our crosses. The Jesus who angered the religious leaders of his day, who ate with prostitutes and tax collectors, who crushed the aspirations of those desperate for a savior who would overthrow the Roman government, is not someone whose work will align well with a modern political platform or overly simplistic economic framework. Jesus was snarky when the religious leaders thought he should be serious, he was compassionate when they thought he should be judgmental, he was sleeping when his followers thought they were in danger, he was angry in the temple when everyone was conducting business, and most of all he was crucified when he had the power to prevent it.

Peacemaking is neither driving toward divisiveness nor maintaining silence and preserving the status quo. The apostle Paul did write a lot about the need for unity among Christians. But, as Jesus clarifies, our job is to make peace and unity as best we can while knowing that people close to us may still sow division. We know this can also be applied in bad faith to justify divisive behavior for earthly goals. But that is a vulnerability inherent to Christianity that we must embrace rather than swat away. Christianity involves a degree of acceptance of some seeming contradictions, some doubts, and much counterintuitiveness. This is why the New Testament talks much more about growing in maturity and love for one another than just learning all the rules. Therefore, what peacemaking is or is not will primarily depend on context and relationships.

More recently, I have been reacquainted with peacemaking terminology through the Enneagram personality types. For the initiated, I am a 5, the Investigator, who tends to be curious, introspective, and concerned with competency and security (this might explain why I have two doctorates). I have a peer who is a 9, the Peacemaker. One day I made a flippant comment about peacemakers being passive, and I was thankfully corrected. Peacemaking is an intensely proactive commitment. Some of our most notable current or recent peacemakers include Malala Yousafzai, Martin Luther King Jr., Mahatma Gandhi, and Greta Thunberg. Would we call any of those leaders passive? Not only are they proactive, but they are also forces to be reckoned with in their pursuits of peace.

This realization and rebuke alters how I read Jesus' Beatitudes. "Blessed are the peacemakers." *Makers* of peace, not peace*keepers*. Not people who stay silent in pursuit of tense quiet that is not real peace. That is a tall order when we look around the world today. We must also be realistic about the limited potential of economic peacemaking. I live in a part of the country where White supremacists are active and militant. We know some of these groups target power substations to cause more chaos.[5] If we offered these individuals pathways to good-paying jobs, perhaps some would accept. But some of them would likely object to working that living wage job alongside people of color. Ideologies can trump economics. Thus economic peacemaking can't solve every problem, but to address peace and reconciliation issues collectively, more people need to be economically thriving. I believe that we are reaching a tipping point of people who might choose violence out of fatigue and hopelessness because they simply cannot reliably make ends meet.

Many Christians find that they are already doing peacemaking in their communities. Making peace is a natural result of following the command to love God and to love our neighbor as ourselves. Loving someone means getting to know them and understanding what they need rather than just giving them what we think they should have. If you go through that process with a person or a community, you will uncover various resources, obstacles, and opportunities. Then, if you do this work of loving your neighbor long enough, you start to see some of the same obstacles or some of the same underutilized resources or opportunities. Large numbers of domestic violence survivors may be struggling financially and get into relationships that turn abusive. Many people in the community may have low credit scores or no credit history. Significant percentages of youth might report poor mental health and suicide ideation, an alarming number of households might be spending more than 50 percent of their income on rent, and so on.

Eventually, you come to ask the bigger question: Why am I loving my neighbor one person at a time when each person seems to have the same problem? It is one thing to help a dad find a job that empowers him to care for his family and be a positive example to his children. But why are so many families struggling to make ends meet? Why is it so hard to help them thrive when many are willing to do whatever is necessary to accomplish that goal? Isn't the best way to love my neighbor to go "upstream" and prevent this problem from being an issue for everybody in the first place? That is how we start to think like economic peacemakers.

CONFRONTING IDOLATRY AND GREED

Many Christians can agree that North American Christianity is in upheaval, although we may disagree on why and the solutions. After many years in ministry and economic peacemaking, simultaneously working in public service and with Christians, I am convinced that many Christians, especially White American Christians, have overlooked the dangers that Jesus warned us about regarding idolatry. We have unwittingly embraced some idols.

Idolatry is tricky. We like to look for Satan working out in the open, blatantly flouting God's values. That's not how it appears to work much of the time. Idols can start out mirroring Christian values and then slowly ask us to make more and more compromises. Over time, we either dare to realize we've strayed and repent, or we must justify behaviors that contradict our stated values. One well-known example is the sale of indulgences in the Catholic Church, which led in part to the Protestant Reformation. What started as calls to pray and give to the church became monetary penalties to absolve sins or spring loved ones from purgatory. During the twentieth century, Adolf Hitler famously won over many Christians through an ideology called "positive Christianity." The Nazis proactively used Christian imagery and symbols, negotiated with the Vatican, and demonized Jews as well as atheist communism. Some German Christians saw through this and resisted, including the theologian Dietrich Bonhoeffer, who was hanged for plotting to assassinate Hitler. But the Nazis rose to power on public—and broadly Christian—favor.

This inside-out idolatry has been a weakness of Christianity from the start, hence the Pauline letters, many of which can be summed up as "Hey, you church, stop that. You know better!" Jesus warns about false prophets who will come in sheep's clothing but are really ferocious wolves (Matthew 7:15). Peter observed this problem in the early church as well: "There were also false prophets among the people, just as there will be false teachers among you. They will secretly introduce destructive heresies" (2 Peter 2:1).

I wonder if some Christians came to believe that if we were spiritual enough, we would be immune to this problem. Gnosticism, or the belief in secret or hidden knowledge, emerged in the early Christian church and has been a persistent heresy. Gnostics believe they can reject orthodox Christianity and go with their gut or place their faith in someone who claims special knowledge. In practice, this assumption, too, seems to have opened the door to idolatry. The rise of televangelists and the prosperity gospel is one example. Today, we can replace the rigor, relationship, and discipline of Christianity with a check sent to the right ministry in exchange for financial blessings.

These slippery-slope idolatries are reminiscent of Satan's temptations of Jesus. Satan did not tempt Jesus to disobey God blatantly. He offered something that sounded like Jesus' ministry, but with a few shortcuts and compromises. We seem to have given into this temptation to some degree, and though it is admittedly an oversimplification, the division in the American church that resulted appears to fall along political party lines: For several decades, some Christians have argued that capitalism is God's economic system, so we need to get rid of the government and the markets will solve everything. I am sympathetic insomuch as this argument emerged during the Cold War, which saw a market-based democracy outlast a Communist-orchestrated economy that completely failed. I am less sympathetic when I realize this surge in skepticism about the government occurred just as people of color finally started to attain a measure of equal representation in the United States both politically and economically.

Nevertheless, in the decades after the Cold War, rhetoric about free markets stagnated while Western capitalism evolved into the short-term-oriented monster it has become or revealed itself to be. That's the increasingly neoliberal capitalism we have now: Lower taxes, less regulation, and more control over the government by the markets through super PACs (political action committees) and lobbyists.

I'm interested in the kind of capitalism that brings prosperity and well-being. The problem with capitalism itself is that it is amoral and is unconcerned with violence if it maximizes short-term profit. Proponents of unrestrained markets are right to point out their benefits. No other tool we possess incentivizes the sheer volume of innovation and productivity, and public systems are far too sluggish and expensive to match the output. But capitalism is a fire-breathing dragon. If you regulate it well, you can harness its power to build cities. If you overregulate it, you leave your most powerful resource wasting away in a dungeon. The people will be free from the fire, but they'll suffer from hunger. But if you release the beast hoping to maximize its impact, it will gleefully burn down the whole city. Capitalism does not care whether there might be nothing left to burn, it only wants to maximize the flames, and today. As the *Marketplace* journalist Kai Ryssdal reminds listeners, more of us are seeing that "capitalism doesn't care whether you live or die."[6]

Here's my hundred-year summary of the US economy: Short-term speculation led to a system of regulation after the Great Depression in the 1920s. Loosening that regulation contributed to the Great Recession in the 2000s, when the financial system jeopardized the global economy by selling houses to people with no income and then repeatedly gambling on the housing market. Today, wealth is concentrating at the top, debt is high (household, commercial, and public), budgets are strained, and disinformation will keep us finger-pointing without addressing real issues. The harness is not fully off the dragon yet, but we can all see the smoke in the air, and more dragon is not the solution for putting out the fires.

Some Christians now realize that much like the wisdom in the system of checks and balances of the branches of the US government, a healthy economy requires a free market balanced with an efficient representative government to ensure the economy exists for the people and not the other way around. Other Christians cannot disentangle their faith from that commitment to neoliberalism as God's economic system. The disinformation easily found on social media and cable networks makes it convenient to avoid this problem. But this solution is like when my three-year-old thinks he is invisible because he covers his eyes. The world still sees what we are doing. In the same way that loving our neighbors as ourselves is a great witness to the world, refusing to love our neighbors out of pride, because we can't do so without acknowledging we were wrong about the system in which they are suffering, is a terrible witness. It has thrown the church, especially the American church, into upheaval and decline.

At the root of our idolatry is the terrible hypocrisy that the United States' most grievous sins have always been based on greed, the effects of which we still live with today. Genocide and theft of Native lands, human chattel slavery, disenfranchisement, Jim Crow laws and systemic racism, the embrace and subsequent expulsion of undocumented immigrants, and the many mechanisms that create, reinforce, and enhance wealth inequality are macro examples of greed as the foundational sin for which White American Christianity needs to repent and be reconciled.[7]

I use this term carefully. "White American Christianity" does not refer to every person who is a White American Christian. It is a recognition of overlapping, historically dominant cultures that have led to systemic harms. White culture, men, and Christianity have been dominant in Western countries for a long time. I am a White, heterosexual Christian American man, but I find myself frequently in conflict with White American Christianity. In the same way, many Christians reject Christian nationalism, whereas people who may not be authentic Jesus followers use Christian language and symbols to attain power.

In that first letter to the Corinthians, Paul also addresses squabbling over whether the Corinthians follow Barnabas, Paul, or Jesus. We have similar squabbling in the American church based on whether we accept greed as the foundational American sin. From my perspective, we have a White Jesus and a Brown Jesus.

The historical Jesus was a Brown man from an oppressed community who, as Isaiah prophesied, "was despised and rejected by mankind, a man of suffering, and familiar with pain" (Isaiah 53:3) and who said some truly shocking things about love, weakness, power, and money.

"White Jesus" embodies the political and economic assertions of White supremacy, sometimes to the point of claiming that the historical Jesus was White. White Jesus says neoliberal capitalism is God's economic system, and the poor are poor because of bad choices. Hence, poverty is not a concern of the wealthy, and comparative wealth is not problematic.

Brown Jesus is who we find when we reject cherry-picking and read the whole Bible. This is the Jesus who turned over the tables of the moneychangers in the temple, who ate with prostitutes and sinners, who saved the woman caught in adultery from being stoned by the religious elite, who told the religious leaders to address the planks in their own eyes before they worried about the splinters in others', and who told pretty much every wealthy person who wanted to follow him that they needed to sell their possessions and give it to the poor.

Following Brown Jesus does not ensure distinct, black-and-white rules for living. It requires wisdom, generosity, and empathy. Our hearts and motives matter as much as our actions, hence the command to be "shrewd as snakes and as innocent as doves" (Matthew 10:16). White Jesus is controversial and offensive because we know it is idolatry. Many of the religious leaders were waiting for their own White Messiah who would help them conquer the Romans, but they got the Brown Jesus who told them to give to Caesar what is Caesar's.

Many White American Christians get security from wealth, privilege, and the state even while condemning the state's capacity to provide security to others. I do not presume to represent Brown Jesus' values accurately for every situation, but I know his clear affirmation that the whole of the Old Testament law can be summed up as love God and love your neighbor as yourself (Matthew 22:37–40). I aspire to take up my cross, die to myself, and follow this Jesus. Of course, I have my vices and propensity to worship idols, so I fall far short of this goal. But to the degree I have followed Brown Jesus, it has led me to a deep desire to love my neighbors by asking why it is so profoundly difficult for families to provide food, shelter, and dignity to children and other vulnerable individuals in one of the wealthiest and most advanced countries in the history of the world.[8]

AN ECONOMY FOR PEACE

Especially in the United States, much of our lives revolve around our perceptions of how the economy is doing. That itself is problematic for Christians because it too often ties God's heavenly kingdom to earthly ones, and we are not as good at disentangling them as we would like to think. To the degree we still pay attention to "how the economy is doing," we do so in ways that seem increasingly odd the closer we look. We can pull in or exclude various indicators to support any belief we have about the economy or to use the economy to support a particular political or social position.

Often, especially in mainstream media outlets, we use two measures to determine the health of the economy: the value of the stock market and the unemployment rate. The economy is doing well if the stock market is at record highs. We talk about the declining economy if the stock market comes down in value, even one or two percentage points. When the unemployment rate increases, we wonder if jobs are scarce and the economy is terrible. When unemployment is low, there must be plenty of jobs, and the economy must be doing well!

These metrics do not address issues such as underemployment, such as part-time jobs. In practice, someone who works multiple part-time jobs, for instance, influences our economic metrics while concealing unsustainable trauma and stress. Someone who cannot find one full-time job that pays a living wage might combine two part-time jobs to accumulate enough working hours per week. These jobs often earn close to minimum wage. If the two employers are international retail giants, the low wages mean more money for shareholders, pushing the stock price up. Profit and productivity are high, so according to surface-level data, the economy is doing well.

But anyone working two part-time minimum-wage jobs to make ends meet is not doing well, especially if they have children or other dependents. Children who experience unstable and insecure housing are often undernourished and stressed and anxious, with fatigued and frustrated parents who are likely to be experiencing other abuse as well. These children are more likely to grow up wounded and unprepared for a complex economy in which earning enough to thrive is increasingly out of reach. Would we be shocked if there were a correlation between this dynamic and the pervasive fear and nihilism that many feel about the future and whether it will be peaceful?

In this book, I talk a lot about a "living wage"—aka a family wage or thriving wage. But what does that mean? There is no definitive and perfectly clear answer to that question, especially not one that endures. Financial coaches and community economic development professionals typically consider a living wage to translate to the ability to afford an entry-level, two-bedroom apartment without spending more than 30 percent of your income on rent. "Entry-level" refers to the cheapest apartments in a community. However, as we will see, 30 percent is a hotly debated ratio. Entry-level apartments are often unsafe, in bad school districts, far from higher education programs, or far from jobs that pay a living wage.

A living wage is distinct from a minimum wage, which tends to dominate conversations about wages. A living wage is a moving target based on the cost of living in a community. The minimum wage can be set by the federal, state, or city government. Currently, the federal minimum wage is $7.25 an hour. Many states have minimum wages ranging from $11 to $16 an hour. There is a movement to push states to adopt a $15 minimum wage. That is all well and good, but higher wages often means prices go up, negating the increased earnings. I prioritize blowing past whatever the minimum wage might be and matching income to life goals and values.

The most important challenge to building a common definition of a living wage job is the disparity between organizational expectations and the aspirations of people living in low-income communities. In marginalized communities with a history of discrimination or systemic disadvantage, households are acutely aware of historical practices like redlining and racially restrictive deeds and housing laws. Redlining—the practice of withholding loans or insurance from neighborhoods perceived to be poor economic risks—continues to have an impact today. Many Black families, for example, were not allowed access to mortgages, whereas many White families across socioeconomic brackets bought homes and accumulated intergenerational wealth. Many people in all communities aspire to buy a home that they can pay off in their lifetimes and pass along to their children as a durable asset. Therefore, a living wage would be sufficient income to meet all your basic needs—including rent or a mortgage payment—while having some disposable income and flexibility to save for a down payment or other major home expenditures, put some money in a retirement account, and take a vacation now and then.

I accept no less for myself, yet even I find myself balking at the difficulty of achieving that goal. This is why we so often default to connecting people with low-wage jobs and hope the situation somehow resolves. However, lowering our expectations for the wages we think people can attain lowers our expectations and aspirations for communities. Our low expectations might lead us to say a living wage job is $18 an hour when a living wage job from a low-income family's perspective is at least $30 an hour. This is true where I live in Tacoma. We are proficient at helping people earn $2 more per hour than the minimum wage, but we avoid the hard conversation about what a living wage is and what it would take for families to attain such a job. What a living wage job is in any given community is up to many factors, but it should be realized and defined within the context of a trusted relationship across communities.

To be clear, peacemaking is not the pursuit of utopia. As a Christian, I believe in sin and fallenness. I do not believe we can attain heaven on earth. The best we can hope for is a dirty mirror reflection of that heavenly kingdom. We will not eliminate selfishness, greed, and violence. But we can be realistic about them and keep them in check in pursuit of loving our neighbors and letting communities live a dignified existence that honors the truth that they are made in the image of God.

There is much work to be done in pursuit of peace, but the overall effort is at risk when someone working multiple jobs cannot pay rent or when a one-time emergency like a car breakdown means they fall behind on rent and cannot get caught up. When a tipping point of the population experiences chronic poverty—or fatigue from flailing to avoid extreme poverty—the fragile peace we are working toward is at risk.

In addition to providing perspective about economic peacemaking and raising empathy for struggling households, this book offers practical strategies for Christians and faith-based communities. Economic peacemaking often includes a range of activities:

- Working with people in the community to understand what a living wage is in any particular region based on the local jobs and socioeconomic factors.

- Similarly, working with community leaders and households to understand how they define a thriving community. This vision might differ from an outsider's assumptions, so the community's priorities must inform an economic peacemaking strategy.

- Gathering and sharing stories about how and why households are struggling to make ends meet, which includes helping disparate stakeholders understand where they unknowingly share values.

- Networking with employers and economic development organizations to understand what living wage opportunities do, or might,[9] exist and what competencies or certifications are required to take advantage of those opportunities. Churches should not overlook how much of this expertise might be already sitting in their pews.

- Networking with higher education institutions, including workforce development agencies and community and technical colleges.

- Cultivating trust that opens the door to communicate this information to households who need it.

- Being prepared to hear and learn about obstacles those households face to take advantage of these pathways, many of which may not have occurred to someone in a different context, and direct ministry efforts to help families overcome these obstacles.

- Adding your voice to the efforts to advocate for systems change based on what you learn, and intentionally doing so without getting pulled into divisive politics.

These practices don't necessarily unfold in a certain order—this is less a checklist and more a rhythm or approach. Still, this should feel like a straightforward and common-sense strategy because it is. Economic peacemaking is highly relationship-based, and doing it with excellence mirrors the types of ministries that churches and Christian organizations have always executed enthusiastically.

The most common questions I am asked about economic development and peacemaking are "What if I am not a math person?" and "What if I am not already an economist or in this field in some way?" The purpose of this book is not to point more math-oriented people at communities, although that would be a fine outcome. The purpose is to equip current or aspiring peacemakers who approach this work with intellectual curiosity and a desire to love their neighbors for the obstacles and opportunities they will inevitably encounter.

You might be thinking, I don't really care about living wage jobs, I am passionate about women and children, anti-trafficking, getting youth into the arts, and so on. That may be where you start. But eventually you will start asking why so many children are accumulating adverse childhood experiences, why survivors of trafficking struggle to be self-sufficient and thrive, and why the youth do not have time or resources to attend your arts activity. The answer will almost always include the realization that somebody, somewhere, needs a living wage job, or this other thing will just not work. I believe that all Christians, at least to some degree, need to be economic peacemakers.

Waging peace with money is not for the passive or the faint of heart. It is messy, ambiguous, and imperfect. Saints will be called heretics, and fools will be celebrated for their criticisms and simplistic solutions. And yet, what it means to be like Jesus in the world and to love our neighbor has never been clearer. The world is watching, and we should lean into Jesus' promise in John 14:12 that whoever believes in him will do the works he did and even greater things.

DISCUSSION QUESTIONS

1. Where might economic peacemaking enhance an existing ministry or program in your community?

2. Who is someone in your community you would consider to be a peacemaker? How are their behaviors or attitudes distinct?

3. What is the economic context of your community? Do you know what a living wage is and which jobs or employers offer at least a living wage? What might be the next steps to learn more?

2

DEVOURED HOUSES

Shame is some tricky [stuff], ain't it? Makes you feel like you want to change, and then beats you back down when you think you can't.
—Walon, in *The Wire*

The rent eats first.
—Matthew Desmond, *Evicted*

In my years of financial coaching and workforce development, I kept hearing a similar story that caused me to doubt the wisdom of using the value of the stock market and the unemployment rate as our primary indicators for the health of the economy.

I remember one man for how perfectly his story illustrated the situations I encountered. He had been a senior commercial truck driver for a local shipping company, earning $28 an hour before the Great Recession. During that recession, around 2009, all the employees agreed to take a pay cut to prevent layoffs. This driver's hourly pay went down to $20. A few years later, a national shipping conglomerate bought this local company. The headquarters of the new employer was out of state, so there were no local relationships and negotiations to be had. They assumed this was the going rate for senior drivers in this region. When we met for a financial coaching session in 2017, he was still earning $20 an hour, but the employer was celebrating substantial profit margins and the company's stock price was higher than ever. Technically, this situation made the economy "better" according to our two metrics. He was working full-time, contributing to a low unemployment rate. His company's stock value was high, contributing to record-breaking wealth for shareholders. But this senior commercial driver was making $8 an hour less than nearly a decade prior. We could not make his budget work with that income, so we started looking for other driving jobs in the area, which was devastating for him.

In low-income communities where I do most of my grass-roots community work, struggling parents often piece together two or three part-time jobs to make ends meet. This is a significant challenge because schedules are often fluid and unpredictable for part-time employment in sectors such as retail, but many parents find ways to make it work. These workers are contributing significantly to the "health" of the economy. They work many hours, and the companies they work for experience high levels of profit and productivity. Since they have jobs, they contribute to a lower unemployment rate. But do they feel economically well? Or, for that matter, physically and emotionally well?

A WIDOW'S MITE-Y REBUKE

As an adult, I read the Bible very differently than when I was a kid. Perhaps that is a disadvantage and I have lost some of my childlike faith. But some stories resonate with me in ways they couldn't when I was younger. Like the story of Jesus praising the poor widow who put all the money she had, two copper coins, into the temple treasury. Thanks to accumulated experience and the insight of others, I've realized that the widow's offering is more subversive and outrageous than I once thought.

This story takes place in Mark 12:41–44. Jesus tells his disciples that this woman gave out of her poverty. I had always heard this story as one about faith and generosity. The wealthy gave much, yes, but they still had more than enough to live on. The poor widow gave everything she had. Where are we on that sliding scale of faith and generosity? I have kids and a mortgage, so I probably won't (or don't have the faith? to) give *everything*, but maybe I'll be a little more generous and try to push myself a little closer to the poor widow's example. And that interpretation is fair if you isolate those verses, as I always had.

But right before this passage, Jesus warns his disciples, "Watch out for the teachers of the law. . . . They devour widows' houses and for a show make lengthy prayers. These men will be punished most severely" (Mark 12:38–40). Jesus tells us to beware the religious leaders who devour widows' houses, and then Mark goes right into a story about a widow experiencing poverty surrounded by wealthy religious men. This isn't just a story about how faithful this woman was; it is a scathing rebuke of the religious community.

Was this poor widow one of the ones who was taken advantage of and whose resources were plundered, a portion of which was then given to the temple to, you know, justify the devouring in the first place? Maybe some of the religious men and legal experts could have given something to the poor widow instead of just to the temple. Perhaps some of them could have done with having a little less wealth in the first place and encouraged the widows in the community to retain what they needed to meet their needs. The widow's mite is both a rebuke of systemic forms of exploitation and a reminder that the systems we participate in might be exploitative.

DEVOURED COMMUNITIES

We face the same exploitative cycle of religious (and other) leaders and devoured houses today. I have been privileged to serve as both funder and funded, wearing various hats and seeing how our social systems work and what is happening to families in various circumstances. Our poor widows today—including trafficking survivors; sexual assault survivors; survivors, especially women and children, of domestic violence; and seniors—are being used up, fixed up, and used again. Some outstanding organizations do comprehensive work for these individuals, often leaving me speechless. They take in someone, often with children in tow, who has survived a traumatic experience. They provide holistic wraparound services, including mental health counseling, access to healthcare, housing, healthy food, legal assistance, advocacy services, and job training. Sometimes these costly but underfunded services last for several years. Then an individual or household can finally step out independently and get an apartment and an entry-level job.

The job training these organizations can offer often leads to jobs such as cashier, entry-level warehouse, home health aide, stocking shelves, and so on. All good and necessary (you know, essential work . . .), but too often minimum wage and part-time. What can a single mom in this situation do?

In financial coaching, our rule of thumb for housing costs is 30 percent of monthly income. Less than 30 percent is considered affordable, 30 to 50 percent is "cost burdened," and more than 50 percent is extremely cost burdened. That final group of households is most at risk of homelessness. As I noted earlier, 30 percent is a hotly debated figure. Depending on other expenses, like childcare and transportation, it might slide up or down. Perhaps someone in a more urban environment can comfortably spend 40 percent of their income on housing because they do not need a car, or their children are old enough to be in publicly funded school and youth programs rather than childcare. But 30 percent is a good way to start a conversation.

As noted, the current federal minimum wage is $7.25 an hour, which is obscene. But in my state of Washington, the minimum wage is $15.74. Let's assume a domestic violence survivor gets a job for $16 an hour. The shorthand for a year of full-time work is 2,080 hours. That's also not realistic, because many entry-level jobs offer closer to 28 hours per week to avoid paying for benefits. Some workers are able to combine multiple part-time jobs, but schedules are often erratic and unpredictable, so this is not always feasible, especially for parents. But let's assume this mom is fortunate enough to get a full-time job or can work two twenty-hour-a-week jobs. That's an annual wage of $33,300 per year.

If we want someone working a full-time job at $16 an hour to pay no more than 30 percent of her income on housing, that is $830 per month. Even at 40 percent spent on housing, that is $1,040. In 2023, rent for a one-bedroom apartment in Tacoma, Washington, averaged $1,300, and a two-bedroom, $1,600.[1] People looking for apartments or housing will tell you those averages are very conservative.

Even if someone can technically afford rent somewhere, they may not be able to access it. Landlords prefer people with excellent credit scores and work histories, which survivors of traumatic experiences often have much less opportunity to build.

It is illegal for landlords to discriminate against someone for being a survivor of domestic violence or other circumstances. Still, property owners and rentals agencies can do other things to screen out applicants they do not want. They can increase the number of months' rent they require up front. I often hear about landlords requiring three to five months' rent. So even if a survivor can find an apartment she can afford, she will compete with many other people for it, some of whom will have better credit or more cash to put down. She will likely end up paying higher rent, closer to the regional average, for something not as nice or safe as an average apartment.

Someone for whom we all have sympathy and want to succeed and thrive, who was blessed to find a $16-an-hour full-time job, might quickly find herself spending 50 to 60 percent of her income on rent. After taxes, transportation, food, clothing, and toiletries, and if she completely avoids things like entertainment for and with her children, she may get by month to month. But it only takes one medical emergency, car breakdown, or temporary loss of income if she does not have paid sick leave. Then she might be compelled to bring herself and her children back into a risky situation. Maybe it's reentering trafficking, moving in with a new partner who turns out to be abusive, or just becoming homeless and either couch-surfing—living temporarily with family or friends—or living in a car, leaving her and her family vulnerable to trauma and abuse. Then, maybe she will mercifully find her way back into one of our outstanding programs again someday.

DEVOURING HOUSES ON A GLOBAL SCALE

Exploitation may have been a much easier problem to solve when you knew who the religious leaders were who were visiting widows and enriching themselves. You could walk up to

them and say, "Stop that!" Today, it seems much more difficult to meet core needs in a community. It can feel as though
external systems are pushing harm into our neighborhoods,
and our local leaders and organizations are struggling to try
to keep up.

Many volumes have been written on the global scale and
diversity of economic exploitation that is devouring houses,
but there are a couple of dynamics in particular we should
understand for community-level economic peacemaking.

Globalization, offshoring, automation, and AI

My community in Tacoma is historically a blue-collar workforce. The city of over 220,000 abuts the Puget Sound about
thirty miles south of Seattle. We have been home to some great
industries related to our thriving port and maritime industries and advanced manufacturing subcontractors associated
with the substantial regional aviation industry. But the same
changes in manufacturing across the country have hit us too.
Many of those facilities have either been moved overseas or to
less union-friendly states by companies looking to maximize
short-term profits (looking at you, Boeing). Or the facilities they
continue to use involve more and more robotics that replace
large numbers of workers. A flood of entry-level healthcare
and retail jobs has replaced higher-wage, middle-class opportunities. You can work at the mall, or a fast-food restaurant,
or you can be a home healthcare aide earning minimum wage.
You might get an entry-level job in one of our many warehouses, but those jobs, too, rarely pay family wages.

Automation that permanently reduces the number of workers, moving factories to states or countries where wages are
low, and technology that allows a global workforce to compete for jobs that used to be local are transforming the nature

of work and wealth. And there are other global trends. Artificial intelligence stands to transform many industries and jobs in ways we do not yet understand. This will likely result in even greater wealth concentrated among a minority, and many more houses devoured as a result.

Limited housing and infrastructure

It's odd to think that just over a decade ago, housing was abundant and relatively affordable. In the early 2000s, easy access to financing had led many households with no or little income to take out loans to buy homes. Eventually, so many households defaulted on mortgages that it triggered a financial crisis that became the Great Recession. Housing prices plummeted, and many people walked away from their homes. Layoffs came in waves, and not enough people had stable income to purchase the homes that were newly on the market. But if you had money, it was a great time to buy up units. Wealthy individuals and corporations did just that.[2]

At the same time, employment and investment in construction lagged for so long that when the economy grew healthier and jobs became more plentiful, the demand for housing was so extreme that prices increased dramatically. In many communities, out-of-state corporations own much of the rental housing. They often charge the highest rents the market will bear, even if those rents are far higher than local wages can afford.

Fortunately, in recent years more housing developments have begun, but it takes a while for them to become available. Larger multifamily units are particularly slow to complete, so in another five or ten years, increased housing stock may take some pressure off prices. Then again, jobs are often concentrated in cities with zoning policies that prevent housing from being built to be close to good jobs.

Housing affordability is less of a burden if you already own a home. But minority households and neighborhoods have historically been excluded from doing so. These neighborhoods often have less investment in infrastructure, are further away from training programs and healthcare facilities, and have less investment in local schools because of lower property values. This adds up to disproportionate vulnerability as the housing prices increase, leading to displacement, often even further away from good jobs and infrastructure.

Financial precarity and expertise

After building some substantial workforce development initiatives that finally connected people in the community with living wage jobs, I noticed a troubling trend. After about a year, some of those folks I had worked with were reaching back out for help and asking about support services, and they were worse off than before they experienced an increase in income. When I started digging into those stories, it began to make sense why. At face value, going from $16 to $24 an hour seems like all your financial problems will be solved. The increase is substantial. For a full-time job, that equates to over $16,000 in annual increased wages. Take out some basic taxes, and that becomes roughly $1,250 in increased monthly income.

What I overlooked was how many urgent needs were waiting to be addressed by people trying to survive on low wages, especially parents. If you are a parent living in a low-income apartment complex, you might always keep your children inside to avoid violence or gangs. Your children's school might be significantly under-resourced, with little education but lots of bullying and other risks. There might be shootings and other physical dangers. So when you get that new job, the priority is to get your children out of there. First, you likely need a car to get to that new job with a higher wage. If you've been taking the bus to your minimum-wage job and don't have personal transportation, you must get a vehicle. Even with a higher income, this isn't easy. With little or no credit, and the promise of more income but no actual savings, you are likely paying $500 to $700 per month for a car payment, and more if you are insured (the sheer lack of insurance among low-income vehicle owners is its own emergency, but we'll hold that thought for now). In all, after paying for transportation needs, the new income coming in each month is already down to something more like $700.

The hunt for a reasonably safe apartment is brutal, especially if you have little or no credit history, have an eviction record, or do not have several months' rent to put down. You are competing with many people who might have good credit and rental history and can put down three to five months' rent. To gain an advantage over other applicants, you might find yourself offering even more per month. But let's assume this person with a fancy new job is granted a lease in a mid-range apartment complex and does not have to put down any extra months' rent. In my community, this probably means you go from paying $1,200 for rent to $1,700 per month. So having a car to get to your new job and moving into an apartment that is not unsafe eats up almost all your new income—and that assumes nothing goes terribly wrong in the hunt for a car and home. And this assumes someone is seeing a $8 hourly increase in wages. This same dynamic plays out when someone sees a $2 or $3 hourly wage increase, which is a much more common outcome.

Many urgent needs have probably gone unmet for this family, sometimes for years. Kids need new clothes, can finally participate in sports or other events, and probably no longer qualify for food assistance. The parent might get medical insurance through the new job but must also pay a premium. They can finally buy birthday presents or Christmas presents. They might buy a computer or a new TV. They sign up for internet access and maybe a term life insurance policy.

These are all excellent outcomes for a family, but they quickly spend more than they bring in. Then the car breaks down or the family has an emergency or health crisis, and they suddenly fall behind. Maybe the car gets repossessed, or rent starts to be late, and things go in the wrong direction. If they lose or can't fix the car, they might lose that new job. Soon after, they're back where they were before the new job, or worse. They might find themselves sitting in my office again, being patient with my struggle to empathize with what happened.

At this point, you might be thinking, This is just everyday life in the middle class. Most people worry about money and the future even if they make a good living, so what is the goal here? You would be correct, but the education, practice, and conditioning required to achieve relative stability are easily overlooked. Low-income families are famously much better at managing and tracking where every penny goes than mid-dle-class and wealthy households.[3] Still, it requires a unique skill set to thrive in these other socioeconomic statuses. And it requires that any supportive organizations understand the reality of households who have faced long-term financial pre-carity. Increasing wages must be paired with other resources, such as mentorship and financial coaching. When these ser-vices are proactively bundled and accessible, outputs start to become outcomes and we get closer to sustainable solutions.

LEARNING TO SEE DEVOURED HOUSES

In the days of widows and temple offerings, it's possible that exploitation was more explicit and thereby easier to address.

In a not-quite-so-globalized world, perhaps it was easier to see the cause and effect: "Hey, that family used to have some wealth, then the husband died, the religious leaders started visiting his widow, now the widow is poor, and the religious leaders seem pretty wealthy." But even when systems that are larger than any one community affect the socioeconomic situation in those communities, you can still learn to read the signs. When an international shipping company buys up all the local family-owned trucking companies, or when a corporation shuts down a factory and moves it to another country, you can see the devoured houses and poor widows that result.

Impossible math for families and seniors

Most financial coaching sessions involve telling the client they need to increase their income. But as we've seen, a lower-income person seeking help rarely has much waste to cut from their budget. They are already accounting for every dollar coming in.

There are some things we can do. Depending on the context, someone might use all their money on necessary expenses, but they have a very high-interest car loan because their credit score could be better. In that scenario, we can work on a longer-term plan to increase their credit scores so they can refinance their loan and decrease their monthly payments, which will free up some income. But that scenario feels like the minority of cases. We can usually find a small amount to cut, but the impact of cutting it out is almost worse than the savings. Perhaps a family's budget deficit is $500 a month and they're spending $100 a month on entertainment, which includes streaming services for the kids and transportation to the library. The family could reduce their deficit by cutting that spending, but is the impact worth the savings?

These are hard conversations, but at the end of them, I can always say, "Look, we need to get your income up. Let's start talking about living wage jobs and pathways and ways to get your income up in the next few months and then on a career pathway to get your wages much higher within the next two to three years."

Some of my most complex financial coaching sessions are with seniors. Many of them have spent their whole lives depending on their physical strength for income. They may receive Social Security and monthly distribution from a modest 401(k), but that often adds up to less than rent, utilities, and food costs. Some may be reluctant to apply for food stamps because they have never had to depend on a service before. In other circumstances, I would emphasize strategies to increase income, but returning to work is rarely an option for seniors, especially if they face physical limitations. I struggle to provide workable solutions. I often make referrals to senior-based organizations and senior-serving organizations. But I also know those organizations call me for advice on how they can help their struggling seniors because they, too, don't know how to support them.

Unaffordable housing and a disappearing lower middle class

In late 2023, while many working households were reporting increases in economic anxiety and rates of credit card and car loan defaults were increasing, American wealth reached an all-time high of $154 trillion.[4] Most of those gains were increases in the value of stocks and real estate. Housing prices were unaffordable across the country, while the wealth of property owners surged.

Part of the problem, and possibly part of the solution, is that our communities have regulated away lower-class housing options. Tacoma's last boarding house finally closed in 2018. It was old and grimy, with small units with tiny kitchenettes and shared bathrooms. A developer bought it, evicted the tenants, and updated it to sell the units as luxury condos. I understand the thought process for legislating away boarding houses. Everyone wants their own bathroom, a decent-sized kitchen, and so on. So cities updated their building codes and building requirements. However, the downside is that these units cost more and take up more space. Eventually, as more luxury and middle-class housing replaced cheaper, denser low-income housing, more people started falling through the cracks. A boarding house apartment might be $400 per month, which someone receiving federal disability benefits might be able to afford.

If someone lives in something akin to a boarding house, it may not be dignified housing, but at least it is stable. Someone who is stably housed is much easier to support through a training program than someone who is unhoused and very likely has developed substance abuse and mental health problems.

Boarding houses are only one example of why we have such an affordable housing problem. We have severe zoning issues. Many communities set aside around 80 percent of their land for single-family homes, and they try to squeeze commercial industry and high-density housing into the few remaining areas. When all that is left in a community are some apartments in extremely high demand for $1,200 per month and a bunch of apartments for $1,600 per month, it should not be a surprise to see rising rates of homelessness. Combine this with the loss of historically middle-class jobs to technology and outsourcing so that more people are trying to afford these rents with minimum-wage jobs, and we start to have the entrenched, complex, expensive problems we face today. Over time, hopelessness starts to seep in, and we begin to lose a vision for peaceful, thriving communities.

It sounds strange, but in addition to more reliable pathways to the middle class, we also need a stable lower-class lifestyle that is not homelessness. This requires not just affordable housing options but rethinking our values and structures about work, consumption, and time. When my wife and I were preparing to return to the United States after living in the Dominican Republic, someone asked us what we would tell people back home about how Dominicans live. They had relatives who had moved to New York and bragged about the fancy buildings and restaurants. But this person knew their relatives were struggling financially and missing home. In the United States, we might have apartments with updated appliances and high-speed internet, but it takes a lot of work to maintain even a lower-middle-class lifestyle. Many communities worldwide have less money, few or no appliances, and no personal transportation, but many have a sense of community and time to spend together.

In the DR, it was challenging to learn to stop being busy and just be with others. No one ever mistook me for anyone but the nerdy White guy I transparently am, but people knew whether I lived there or was a tourist based on some of these behaviors. When we went to a *colmado* (corner store), there were small and jumbo bottles of beer. Only tourists bought small ones for themselves. I never saw a Dominican buy, or drink from, a small bottle of Presidente. You always buy a jumbo bottle with several small plastic cups and sit and share. I also learned to walk to various neighbors' houses, accept coffee, and be there either talking or playing dominos.

In many places in the United States, we have flipped this dynamic on its head. Without a viable lower-middle-class way of living, leisure is for the wealthy. Everyone else has to work multiple jobs and lacks disposable income or energy to build a community. There are few free common spaces where we might get to know our neighbors. The time we might spend with each other is spent on one or more side gigs trying to make ends meet, chasing a dragon we can never catch but knowing that if we stop trying, the alternative may well be homelessness.

Shivering children and other adverse childhood experiences

When it comes to devoured houses, my primary concern is the impact on children and youth. The work of building a financial empowerment initiative, combined with becoming a father myself, has enhanced my perspective in this area.

When building a financial inclusion program for a local nonprofit, I raised enough money to hire seven financial coaches embedded in organizations around the county. But many households did not have a way to get to one of our offices. Not wanting to put my staff at risk, I handled mobile financial coaching sessions myself. I found myself traveling around the county, being invited into people's homes, sitting at their kitchen tables, and having them open their finances to me. The vulnerability required to do this was palpable, and I always tried to respect the courage it took to ask for help in this way.

I remember one typical experience of being invited to some-one's home in the middle of winter. It was a small one-bed-room apartment in a rundown complex in a low-income area. The family invited me in, we sat at the kitchen table, and I started preparing my intake paperwork. The apartment was dark; the electricity had been shut off. This meant no heat, and a young boy was sitting on the couch, wearing a thick coat and covered in a blanket. He just sat, staring at a blank TV, trying to stay warm.

That relationship ultimately ended like many others: I could not make their budget work with the money they brought in. Every penny of their income went to basic needs, and they fell further behind each month. They needed to develop a strategy to increase their income before we could talk about budgets and credit scores. I made an appointment for them with a workforce development agency I trust. But I remember leaving the apartment with that young boy in my mind and thinking, "Well, that can't be a good long-term investment."

We struggle to understand long-term directions and indicators in communities. Are things getting better or worse, or are we at a stage in some intergenerational cycle? Part of the challenge of clarifying how we're doing is related to the complexity of our world and the subjective nature of the answer. But in community development, one of our most reliable metrics is rates of adverse childhood experiences, or ACEs.

ACEs are ten categories of traumatic events: physical abuse, sexual abuse, emotional abuse, physical neglect, emotional neglect, a family member with depression or a mental illness, a family member with an alcohol or substance abuse addiction, a family member in prison, witnessing a parent being abused, or losing a parent to separation, divorce or death. Children who accumulate ACEs are at much greater risk of mental, physical, and emotional challenges as they become adults. Tracking and mitigating the number of adverse experiences children have is critical, as is building resilience in children and ensuring families have sufficient protective factors.

The number of ACEs that children accumulate can vary greatly. Some children in low-income communities experience none, while some children in affluent neighborhoods

accumulate many. Some protective factors, such as safe housing and healthy food, cost money. But studies consistently
show that high levels of poverty correlate with higher numbers
of ACEs.[5]

As with most metrics and indicators, we have limited reliable data. Over the past few decades, some ACE categories
have increased in frequency for children while others have
decreased. It seems that mental health, substance abuse, and
neglect are on the rise.[6] But whether this is about reporting
or destigmatizing versus increases in actual occurrences
is unclear.

Determining what is happening in a community is difficult by simply driving through it. Some cities have an open
and visible issue with economic struggles and addiction; in
others, vulnerabilities are hidden behind closed doors. But
qualitatively speaking, from my experience working at the
grassroots level, ACEs and hopelessness are often correlated.
Parents who are working but falling short each month or who
struggle to find and keep a job can experience shame, which
can lead to neglect or abuse, wearing down all members of a
household and their hope for the future.

ALICE households and the invisible homelessness

More common than someone experiencing homelessness or
extreme poverty are very low-income households that earn
too much money to qualify for help, or are overlooked by
churches and organizations but are at risk of homelessness or
other vulnerable situations. Children in these households are
at higher risk of adverse childhood experiences.

These families are known as ALICE households: asset limited, income constrained, but employed.[7] ALICE is a household
with two working parents, perhaps one working full-time and

one part-time, who bring in approximately $55,000 a year. They might be spending 50 percent or more of their monthly income on rent, and after other basic needs such as utilities, food, gas, car payments, and especially childcare, they are struggling. They do not have enough disposable income to save. If the car breaks down or someone needs to visit the emergency room, they could be in trouble.

Many of us are accustomed to seeing people experiencing homelessness or other people in poverty. But the federal poverty line for one person for 2023 is $14,550, which translates to just under $7 an hour working full-time. As noted earlier, the hourly minimum wage in Washington State is $15.74. Just about anyone can walk into any fast-food restaurant and earn $17 an hour. But that won't go far enough to rent an average apartment in my region. Most households are ineligible for social service benefits if they earn more than 200 percent of the federal poverty level. There were many social service benefits during the COVID-19 pandemic, but as that funding dwindled, we reverted to having few services available besides food subsidies.

A significant risk to these families is the massive rent increases we have seen recently. I have met with families who were already struggling financially and who then received notice that their monthly rent would increase by $200, $300, or sometimes $500. This often forces a family to look for a new home, which requires competing with all the other families struggling to pay increasing rent. Many landlords have increased the number of months' rent up front to filter out the competition and riskier tenants. An ALICE household, not having had any disposable income for years, does not have the $3,000 to $5,000 in upfront costs to move into a new apartment. Families work, fight, and borrow to make these transitions work, but when rents increase, a few more families fall through the cracks.

An ALICE family may be easy to overlook in part because they are not (yet) homeless. A single parent spending 60 percent of her income on rent who has fallen behind on other bills may not currently be homeless, but that family is on that trajectory. It is only a matter of time or a matter of the next car breakdown or illness. Still, they are distinct from families, children, and youth who are already unhoused. I managed the human services department for a small local city for a time. Part of my job became going around the community explaining that we should spend less energy fretting about the tent encampments popping up. Yes, this is a problem we need to deal with. But there is another category of homelessness that is more urgent and which we cannot see on the way to the grocery store.

When families with children become homeless, they are not as likely to pitch a tent on the street. Some go to a homeless shelter, but those are temporary solutions that are often full. Most families either move into their vehicles or start couch-surfing. Often, living in a car will become couch-surfing, especially in extreme weather. It is becoming more common to see one- or two-bedroom apartments with several families squeezed into them. This is also risky because if the landlord discovers this, it can lead to eviction for all the families, increasing the number of households looking for somewhere affordable.

Without a massive investment by the federal government, it is unclear how we will solve the country's burgeoning homelessness crisis. Once someone becomes homeless, they are very likely to acquire a mental health and substance abuse issue regardless of whether they had one beforehand.[8] Providing multiple years of housing and rehab for everyone who needs it would require tremendous time and money.

While we continue working to mitigate homelessness, our communities have many ALICE families. These families are an excellent place for us to invest our resources because we can help those working adults navigate toward better-paying jobs and prevent future adverse childhood experiences for the children and youth in those households. It is much more affordable, has a more straightforward pathway to success, and is one of the best long-term investments in our communities.

There are many other ways we are devouring houses, including the subtle ways we encourage exploitation and lock people into poverty. One complex issue that serves as a good example is work requirements for federal benefits. Most people would agree that someone who can work should do so rather than depend on social services and public funding. However, since the 1996 welfare reform efforts, we have gone too far in the direction of reducing and restricting benefits. The social service system is much less robust, and the available resources have many restrictions and requirements. People must be working to be eligible, and they must be willing to take a job quickly. This makes sense, except in most cases, people are compelled to take poverty-wage jobs. So if someone is not eligible for a social service if they turn down a job, they must take a job even if it pays close to the minimum wage, with which almost no one in the United States can afford rent. Therefore, a system that is supposed to serve as a safety net while people prepare for and seek out good jobs locks people into poverty wages.

Much has been written about the opioid crisis and the billions of dollars in profit from drugs such as OxyContin. Much has been discussed about tipping culture in the United States and the shockingly low minimum tipping wage. Many decry the volume of undocumented workers from whom

Americans receive low-cost goods and services. Parents with young children struggle mightily to make ends meet until their children age into kindergarten or other publicly funded schooling options. Transportation, infrastructure, and schools in low-income communities are chronically underfunded and overlooked. Health insurance is simultaneously costly and unusable due to high deductibles and copayments. How, then, do we proceed?

THE TEMPTATIONS OF JESUS

Over the past few years, I've thought a lot about the temptations of Jesus. When Satan tempts Jesus after forty days in the wilderness, we read about those temptations like we're wondering whether we should have a fourth slice of pizza—we read them from a state of abundance. Jesus was weakened and vulnerable, and Satan tried to cut deep. Historically, my reaction to these temptations is, "Oh, yeah, yeah. Me too, Jesus. I don't need bread or earthly authority or splendor and will not live on bread alone but from every word from God." But that's a lie. I'm a straight, White, middle-class-ish American man. I upgraded to a bigger TV last year because football; I have a hot tub (inflatable, but still); and I have a home office with a leather couch because I can. Can I say I don't live on bread alone when I have a drawer in my office just for protein bars? Many North American Christians struggle with this blind spot, but ignoring this issue prevents us from addressing wealth and peacemaking.

The second temptation (in Luke) deserves special consideration. What exactly is Satan tempting Jesus with here, and are we faced with the same temptation today? The book of Luke describes it as the tempter showing Jesus "in an instant all the kingdoms of the world" (Luke 4:5). If Jesus worshiped

Satan, he would receive all the authority and splendor. Of course, Jesus had the classic response, "It is written: Worship the Lord your God and serve him only" (4:8). The book of Matthew adds to the narrative the iconic "Away from me, Satan!" (4:10).

At first glance, this temptation seems to be wealth and comfort. That would make sense. However, the first temptation is to turn stone into bread—that covers the bases in terms of meeting physical needs and comforts. The third temptation, meanwhile, is to put God to the test. See whether the angels will save you if you throw yourself off the temple, says Satan. But the second temptation, I think, is about worship. Jesus is the king, and Satan is offering him a throne right now that won't require the pain and the sacrifice that is coming. However, we also know Jesus is concerned with the weak and powerless, especially children. If you were someone whose heart breaks for children and you were shown the entirety of the world's kingdoms in an instant, how much pain would you witness at that moment? I wonder if Satan tempted Jesus more than he knew.

The throne is its own temptation, but more importantly, so is what one could do with that throne. Jesus, weak from forty days of fasting and wandering, could snatch up the throne immediately and install his kingdom. He could end child poverty, heal everyone, and establish all the just systems we all thirst for. He could compromise this one time, ask his Father for forgiveness, and declare it spiritual "means to an end." Surely giving in to temptation is okay if he uses that authority and splendor to serve others . . . in addition to that shiny crown . . .

The temptation of authority and splendor. Is this our present temptation? How do we balance attaining the authority and influence to make the economy work for everyone without slipping into politics as idolatry, without worshiping Satan as a means to an end in the name of Jesus?

SEARCHING FOR VILLAINS

We must transition to a discussion about the other side of our economy—those who have way more than they need—but first, we need to acknowledge our tendency to look for evil bad guys to blame and fight. To be sure, many people are selfish, angry, hurting, or have mental health issues, but by and large, there is no villain we can blame for the challenges we face. We are collectively culpable and responsible. I fill my car with gas and pollute the air, buy technology or clothing likely made by children or other exploited workers, buy plastic junk I do not need, and spend money at stores that displace local small businesses. I know I am part of the problem even as I search for solutions. But we cannot let the perfect be the enemy of the good. Engaging with economic peacemaking work means becoming comfortable with saying "I don't know." I pray for us to replace judgment and self-righteousness with empathy and curiosity.

This leads to an essential point about strategy. Reasonable people can debate the ideal approach, but there is no one right answer. The United States is a large country with many people. Either someone will get a benefit they don't need because we are being too generous or someone who really needs help won't get it because we are being too restrictive. Rather than recommend a particular blend at this stage, I would call out our dread of being taken advantage of, which seems to dictate our current skepticism of offering help and support at any scale. This fear collides with the instruction for Jesus followers to "turn. . . the other cheek. . . . And if anyone wants to sue you and take your shirt, hand over your coat as well" (Matthew 5:39–40).

There will always be people unable or unwilling to grind away every day, trying to earn a living in service to the great golden bull of wealth and consumption. We tell narratives about people "not wanting to work anymore," but that seems more like exhaustion from exploitation. You put in extra hours, but you don't get paid for them, and you have to work extra gigs to pay the rent. Every job requires a college degree, so you go to college, but the jobs that require the degree do not pay enough to pay down the student loans. You take risks and innovate at work, maybe increasing efficiency or exploring a new product or service, but the value of that effort goes to shareholders who contribute nothing. You get the same paycheck regardless. Eventually, you start to realize you are not building toward anything. You constantly work but can't get ahead to start the life you want, and you sacrifice mental health, physical health, and community in the process. There is no carrot, but the stick of homelessness looms large and works for a while.

But everyone has a breaking point. A growing number of people are giving up and losing hope. I will fail anyway, they think, so why keep grinding? When too many people fall into that camp, our systems stop working and our communities can't flourish.

We can see this behavior throughout the United States. When there were eviction moratoriums during the pandemic, many people stopped paying rent. They knew they would get evicted when the moratoriums ended, and they weren't necessarily proud about it all, but they knew this was their chance to get ahead. They could finally buy clothes for their kids and replace an old laptop instead of throwing everything at the rent. The consequences would come, and the eviction on their record would haunt them, but maybe it was a chance to break the cycle.

Meanwhile, populist candidates are gaining momentum. They are taking advantage of fatigue and scarcity to convince us that villains are at our doors and must be defeated at all costs. Authoritarians are bad for democracy and bad for a thriving economy. They can only break things and blame others, but even though it's likely to end badly, it's a chance for something different. Something, somewhere, has to give. If we wait too long, something will, and it will probably not be peaceful.

DISCUSSION QUESTIONS

1. Who are the devoured houses in your community?
2. The last thing we want to do is start finger-pointing and accusing one another of being hypocrites and exploiters. So how do you assess your own behavior in this respect?
3. How are children and youth faring in your community? What is the peacemaking trajectory of your community based on this answer?
4. You may not have been wandering in the desert without food for forty days like Jesus did, but perhaps you are (or can recall a time when you were) weakened from years of scarcity of time, money, safety, or health. Which of the three temptations of Jesus (bread, power, testing God) might you be most vulnerable to? How might you respond to the tempter?

THE GOLDEN ~~CALF~~ BULL

The point is, ladies and gentleman, that greed, for lack of a better word, is good. Greed is right, greed works. Greed clarifies, cuts through, and captures the essence of the evolutionary spirit. Greed, in all of its forms; greed for life, for money, for love, knowledge has marked the upward surge of mankind.

—Gordon Gekko, in *Wall Street*

I can't believe you like money too. We should hang out.

—Frito Pendejo, in *Idiocracy*

Most of my peacemaking work has been in and with communities. Over time, I have had more opportunities to work with stakeholders outside of low-income neighborhoods. This provides a unique opportunity to improve communication between groups who may otherwise never interact. The alarming dynamic with doing this work is how often these stakeholders believe they are in conflict and disagreement when, in practice, they are almost entirely on the same page about the community's problems and the ideal solutions.

Each stakeholder has their fair share of simplistic narratives, conspiracy theories, and disinformation, always more than they realize. But when you get past the veil of disinformation, most everyone wants the same thing. Parents want a good and healthy future for their children and will make whatever sacrifices they must to increase the likelihood of that happening. The impoverished and the wealthy worry about crime; both agree that good jobs are an excellent preventative measure against crime and violence, and everyone prefers a dignified and good-paying job to sitting around watching television.

It can be exhausting to go back and forth encountering the same false assumptions and sharing the same empathy-raising stories and values to get people on the same page. But it is also a privilege to help unlock a community's ability to work together to solve complex problems. And generally, everyone is tired of the mud-slinging and online abuse and is thrilled to put down their screens and talk to people in their community. Occasionally, I encounter hypocritical attitudes or people engaged in exploitation who will not compromise their commitment to idolatry.

One year, I engaged with numerous faith communities in a city with surprisingly high rates of extreme poverty and extreme wealth in the same zip codes. I went through the typical process of building trust with a community, attending community meetings, and looking for opportunities to show good faith and achieve quick wins. I was concerned about the meager incomes in two zip codes and watched the monthly trends of skyrocketing housing costs. I wanted to discuss housing and jobs, but that's not how you start. I listened, and at one meeting, they talked about a disintegrating corkboard in the center of the community that was critical for neighborhood communication. Many households did not have home internet, so this physical information-sharing tool was essential. I used some discretionary funds to replace the corkboard, and at the next meeting I attended, attendees started opening up about more profound anxieties. They could also see the rising housing rates and were frustrated that no one was building more affordable housing. I listened and explained everything being done to encourage housing construction. There was a lot of regional demand for construction projects and materials. So even if we removed all affordable housing requirements, we would still struggle to attract companies away from lucrative projects in bigger cities.

Over time, this led to conversations and grieving over the state of things. Eventually, we started talking about jobs and some exciting programs at a local technical college that I was confident would lead to living wage jobs. Community stakeholders shared some of their concerns about these programs. Even a one-year program takes a lot of work. Many of these programs are unlike business degree programs that can be done online and in the evenings. Program participants would have to be on campus regularly, get to and from the campus, and somehow afford rent, food, and diapers along the way. It was unclear how we would overcome all these logistical challenges, but we were working through it, and there was hope.

Simultaneously, I met with church leaders in wealthier parts of the community. Many of them were sympathetic and eager to help. I suggested we figure out a way for churches to "adopt" families going through training programs that we were confident would lead to living wage jobs. This was progressing well, and we identified a local nonprofit as the hub for future conversations and coordinating such an effort. However, one large and wealthy church community did not want to meet with me. As our work ramped up, someone from that church finally contacted me and invited me to attend a ministry meeting. A couple of weeks later, I showed up, without a particular plan or goal other than to listen, build some trust, and answer any questions they might have about the initiative.

It turned out it was essentially an intervention. They told me that I was spreading heresy and had been deceived by Satan. In that moment, I felt that trying to defend or explain myself would only cement their opposition to my work, so when there was a lull, I thanked them for their time and passion and said I would like to remain in conversation with them. The meeting then ended with a prayer. The prayer included, among other things, an appeal to God to protect the stock market and grow it despite the liberals and the liberal state that wanted to steal from hardworking Americans. That was the last time anyone from that church wanted to meet with me.

THE GOLDEN CALF

When I think about the story in Exodus 32 of Moses on Mount Sinai and the Israelites turning to idol worship, I realize I recall the story incorrectly. I remember a more straightforward narrative: Moses went up the mountain into the pillar of smoke, God gave him the Ten Commandments on the two stone tablets, the Israelites made a golden calf almost immediately after Moses was out of sight and started worshiping it, and Moses smashed the tablets in disgust when he came back down the mountain. The story can be tidily told in the span of a Sunday school hour.

But the story is not so simple.

First, Moses did not just ascend the mountain one time. He ascended multiple times. He brought a wealth of information and context back to the people. It is hard to ignore the modern relevance of the laws given to the Israelites before they turned to golden idols over which they might have more control. In addition to keeping the Ten Commandments, they were not to oppress foreigners (Exodus 22:21), take advantage of widows or the fatherless (22:22), charge interest to people in need (22:25), spread fake news (23:1), deny justice to poor people in lawsuits (23:6), among others. This list raises an eyebrow in today's context, and one wonders whether these restrictive rules affected the people's haste to start crafting an idol that might be more open to exploitative opportunities to accumulate wealth.

Second, the transition to idol worship was much more of a slippery slope than I realized as a kid. The Israelites did not immediately start worshiping the golden calf, although they did ask Aaron for gods to go before them. Their faith was weak; they were terrified by the pillar of smoke consuming the mountain, and Moses was not there to reassure them constantly. So Aaron melted down gold from the people and fashioned the infamous golden calf. Then, after acknowledging that this gold was the gods who brought them out of Egypt, Aaron said, "Tomorrow there will be a festival to the LORD" (Exodus 32:5). Yikes!

We can't have it both ways. We can't establish a golden idol, put our faith in that idol to comfort ourselves because we're anxious, and then smooth out all the contradictions by being spiritual and acknowledging the one true God. "No one can serve two masters," said Jesus. "Either you will hate the one and love the other, or you will be devoted to the one and despise the other. You cannot serve both God and money" (Matthew 6:24). The Lord who brought the Israelites out of captivity is a jealous God. God will not share the spotlight with a golden idol.

In a book that seeks to equip more Christians to enhance their ministry work with economic development and an emphasis on living wage jobs, this argument might seem ironic. I believe this is a good example of living "shrewd as snakes and innocent as doves" (Matthew 10:16). We need to think about money, jobs, wealth, the economy, and the stock market as we think about ministry programs and what it means to love our neighbors as ourselves. But we must also be wary of our inherent weakness to put our faith and hope in golden idols, whether literal sculptures or economic structures. Today, we may not be tempted by golden calves, but our world is often bent in service of the great bull of Wall Street.[1] We must be wise enough to emphasize jobs and money but innocent enough to keep ourselves untarnished by idolatry. I do not do that perfectly, nor do you, but thankfully, we serve a forgiving God who will accomplish great things with our imperfect labor.

MEET PAUL AND SAMANTHA

To better understand how varying contexts can put people who share values and alignments into conflict, let's consider the stories of two individuals who live in the same community. For the sake of privacy, they are each composites of real people and dynamics I've encountered in my work and social worlds.

Paul

Paul is a retiree in his late seventies. His three grown children have their own families. Paul worked in construction his whole career. He married at a young age, and he and his wife had children immediately. He worked hard and physically pushed himself daily to provide for his family. They bought a house and felt solidly in the middle class. Paul worked long hours and took extra shifts and jobs whenever he could. He didn't get to see his kids as often as he liked, but his primary responsibility was to provide for his family, so that's what he did.

The physical labor started to take a toll in his forties. Paul worried about how many more years he needed to work relative to what his body could handle, and he wanted to help get his kids through college. At the same time, many of Paul's peers owned construction companies and were growing wealthy without performing the hard labor themselves. The value of the house he and his wife had bought had grown, and they were sitting on a lot of equity. Paul took out a home equity loan drawn from the value of the house and started his own company. Shortly after, a downturn in the market affected the construction industry, among others.

The economy recovered quickly, but the timing was terrible for Paul's new company. In addition to equipment and costs associated with his startup, he used some of his home equity money to pay the monthly bills. Eventually, the money ran out, Paul sold his equipment for a little less than what he had purchased it for, and he got his old job back. He refinanced his home loan and absorbed the home equity loan into a new thirty-year mortgage. His monthly payments were much larger. This was all very stressful for Paul and his family. Paul was always gone, always working, always taking extra shifts or working overtime whenever possible. When he was home, he was visibly frustrated and anxious. Everyone knew why; no one held a grudge, but it was hard. Everyone knew to leave Dad alone.

A few years later, all the kids had their own homes or were away at college. Paul and his wife were empty nesters, but they discovered they no longer knew each other. Eventually, they decided to divorce, and Paul's wife moved out and got a job. Paul didn't need the house all to himself and was struggling with the monthly payments, so he put it on the market. When the house sold, Paul paid off the mortgage. He didn't have enough left over to buy something else. He purchased a newer car to replace the old one he had been driving for many years and invested the rest in a small 401(k) retirement account. He found an affordable rental unit and hoped to keep working as long as possible.

By his sixties, Paul had to give up the construction jobs. His body could not handle the workload. All the jobs he could find required four-year degrees and computer skills. He transitioned to working in warehouses for a while, but the physical demands of that job caught up with him as well. He got a part-time job in retail that didn't pay very well, but it didn't require him to be there forty hours a week and it wasn't physically demanding. Paul was nearing retirement age and growing concerned. He no longer owned a home, and he didn't have any savings. The amount in his 401(k) was modest, and he wanted to wait until he was seventy to retire and start drawing Social Security, since benefits increase if a retiree waits until then.

Other things had changed while all this was happening, some without Paul realizing. He used to read the newspaper and watch the news on television. It was a great way to stay informed about what was going on in the world while also being distracted from the daily grind. But behind the scenes, the local newspaper had shut down, and the local television news network was purchased by a national conglomerate that mandated a particular political perspective. The national news he could find was the same talking heads with boxy graphics Paul was used to, although the rhetoric was getting angrier and more political. But it looked like the news, so that must be what it was.

Paul didn't have much computer experience, but his children helped him buy a smartphone so they could send him pictures of his grandchildren. The same tools on the phone to view those photos also provided access to news, and those news sources were talking about Social Security and the stock market. These were Paul's only real assets. Apparently, someone was trying to take those away from him. So Paul started spending more time on his phone, going where those narratives led.

Samantha

Samantha is in her early twenties. She graduated from college a little over a year ago and is struggling to make ends meet. Her parents never went to college, but they were determined that Samantha would. They worked low-wage jobs, usually multiple ones, to ensure that Samantha would have opportunities that previous generations of her family never did. However, her parents could not help with college tuition. Samantha was accepted to a state college several hours away from home. She took out student loans to cover her tuition and pay for her on-campus housing. For the first couple of years, Samantha didn't worry about this. She even took out some private student loans in addition to her federally subsidized loans. She knew the narrative. She understood that the days of working part-time to pay for college so you could graduate debt-free were over, but that was fine. College was more expensive now, so you borrow money, but you make so much more from having a four-year degree that it more than pays for the loans and interest over time.

But by Samantha's junior year, she was losing confidence. She wasn't being irresponsible. She went out occasionally but ate all her meals using her mandatory campus housing meal plan. She didn't replace her computer, upgrade her phone, or go on vacation during breaks. But for some reason, the debt was piling up and the private loans were accumulating interest, and she still had two years of school left. She got a part-time job in the evenings and weekends, but it paid minimum wage and seemed like a drop in the bucket compared to the ballooning loans and monthly expenses. She took extra classes that year and worked through the summer so that she could graduate in December of her senior year, saving her from taking out more loans for that final semester. What else could she do? This is what college cost at a state college—and it was much more affordable than the private colleges that many of her friends attended. And people who did not attend college had no shot at the middle class, right?

Now that she's out of college, Samantha feels like she has a mortgage, which is not far off. She has more student loan debt now than her parents owned on their first home mortgage. But that doesn't mean anything. Everything was more affordable then, and wages were lower, so you can't compare. Samantha has also discovered two other realities. First, the cost of housing is extreme. Second, while a college degree is required to get any job, most everyone applying for any job also has a degree. A college degree is needed to obtain a job that pays a little better than one that does not require the degree, but it does not make you competitive for a great job, because so many other people have degrees. It also seems like the great jobs are few and far between. Samantha heard only rumors and legends about people like her getting a job that allowed them to pay down some principal on their student loans, not just the interest!

Samantha's parents suggested saving money by renting a studio above someone's garage. That sounded lovely and restful, but all the garage studios Samantha could find charged as much as a one-bedroom apartment and had dozens of applicants. Samantha currently rents a room in a two-bedroom apartment in a suburb of a city where good jobs can be found. Even though rent eats almost half her take-home pay, she doesn't need to buy a car, because there is a direct bus to the city. The places further out might be more affordable to rent, but that would be too far to compete for any good jobs.

Samantha hopes that if she can hold on long enough with a good job, it might lead to a great job that allows her to pay down her student loans and start her *real* adult life. Sometimes, Samantha goes out on the weekends, but during the week, she works, commutes to her rented bedroom, and stays in to save money. Much of that time is spent on her phone and streaming TV shows, trying to squeeze some rest from the stressful days and longing to get out from under the crushing weight she feels.

While scrolling on her phone, she sees videos and photos of other people her age traveling, parenting, smiling, and living their best lives. She also perceives frustration among older generations that something is wrong with her generation. They're not starting families or buying homes at the same rate as previous generations. They don't seem to care about the stock market or express an appreciation for capitalism. Samantha is confused by this frustration. No jobs she has applied for offer pensions or a matching 401(k) contribution. She's primarily worried about student loans and finding a job that offers a healthcare plan; she's not considering retirement. She's got to get out from under that weight before she can think about kids or a mortgage.

Unwitting division

Paul and Samantha seemingly don't have much in common, and though they don't know each other, they are part of the same church community. Paul longs for social connection, and the neighborhood church is smaller but friendly. They have some excellent volunteer programs. Paul helps serve meals and distribute donated clothing on Thursdays. He always attends the Sunday morning sermon and enjoys connecting with other seniors who attend. Samantha usually goes out with friends on Saturday evenings and sleeps on Sundays. She dislikes the traditional Sunday church service that feels like the meetings she must attend for work each week, but she loves being part of a Wednesday night small group affiliated with the church.

One day, a hostile foreign government creates a social media post to foster division. It's gaudy and audacious. This particular meme is a figment of my imagination, but you've likely seen something like it online: President Biden is wielding a sword with *Socialism* inscribed on the hilt; he is using it to decapitate the iconic *Charging Bull* on Wall Street, and there is a faint hint of a Satanic tail flowing from the president's suit. Many AI bots promote the image and post both sarcastic and supportive comments.

Paul is scrolling on social media, sees the post, and reads the comments. He is unaware that a foreign government created this image and is unfamiliar with the concept of bots meddling with social media posts. It looks like the clever political cartoons he used to see in printed newspapers. This image reinforces the information he gets from his phone. He is inundated daily with articles, videos, and pictures that will strengthen the idea that capitalism is God's economic system and America is God's chosen country. The American flag is the same as the Christian cross. Socialism isn't clearly defined, but whatever it is, it's Satan's work, and the younger generation has fallen for it. They're lazy and wasteful, and in their sloth, they're turning God's system that Paul contributed his whole career to over to Satan. Meanwhile, immigrants are pouring over the US-Mexico border, and they also buy into Satan's systems. God's economic system and country must be defended from whatever socialism is. Paul sees this image on social media and sees what appear to be other people like him reveling in it. He copies it and goes to another app on his phone just for neighbors to interact with each other, and he gleefully reposts it there.

The image does not appear in Samantha's social media feed. Hers contains pictures and videos depicting the fabulous wealth that older generations have accumulated from owning shares in banks that purchased lucrative student loans, buying up rental properties, and raising rents much higher than local wages can afford. She also spends time on the neighborhood app and sees Paul's post since she lives in the same area. She doesn't know Paul, but she assumes he must be one of those wealthy older gentlemen who has accumulated plenty of wealth by exploiting the ambition of people like her to get into the middle class. This post catches her on a particularly tiring day, so she responds with an angry comment. She regrets posting it a few minutes later and logs back on to delete it, but people have already responded with vitriol. Paul reacts as well, and he and Samantha get into a heated virtual exchange that both will regret and feel shame over later. To the degree there is substance in their exchange, part of what they fight about is their relative allegiance to the stock market. They have accomplished nothing, but the hostile foreign country has achieved its goal, and both Paul and Samantha have unwittingly participated in the sowing of division in the church.

I will not pretend to be a psychologist who understands precisely what happens when we engage strangers in the digital atmosphere. But the result of these conflicts, like so many other conflicts over class and inequity, is leaving an imprint.

Tribalism so often leads to fear, which makes us vulnerable to idol worship. We long for an Aaron to give us some semblance of the old tangible gods. Samantha and Paul may have started with the stock market as a tool or a part of society that they understood to varying degrees and maybe felt some connection to. But with every divisive, frustrating interaction, it becomes a symbol increasingly wrapped up in their identities. White American Christianity has a greed problem that leads to an idolatry problem. Making peace starts with seeing the idols for what they are, repenting, seeking reconciliation, and choosing to do better, somehow, moving forward.

DIAGNOSING GREED

How do we know we have an acute greed problem in the United States today? There are many stories and data points, but I want to examine a few of the primary factors in today's economy—including the size of the stock market relative to gross domestic product, the concentration of wealth, the trajectory of wages, the proliferation of corporate lobbyists and loosened campaign finance rules, tax rates, and government spending and debt. All of these are complex topics that warrant greater study, but to start, a shared understanding of these factors can help inform economic peacemaking strategies that lead to the outcomes we want.

The stock market versus GDP

When we talk about the stock market, we're often talking about a stock market index—the Dow Jones Industrial Average, the S&P 500. These indexes represent large swaths of the markets where investors buy and sell shares of company stock. The overall value of the stock market is typically understood to represent the value of future economic activity. Gross domestic product, meanwhile, does not perfectly capture all the economic activity in a country, but it is a helpful metric to assess the size of an economy. GDP is a broad measure of a nation's economic activity and includes the total value of goods and services produced. It can overlook the underground economy, such as services provided for cash, or unpaid labor, such as parenting, but it is our best crude tool to measure the economy.

Comparing the size of the stock market to GDP, also known as the Buffet Indicator (after businessman Warren Buffet), gives us a sense of whether the stock market is overvalued or undervalued.[2] It can be difficult to know what to do with this indicator. Perhaps a highly valued stock market means that publicly traded companies are innovating at such a pace

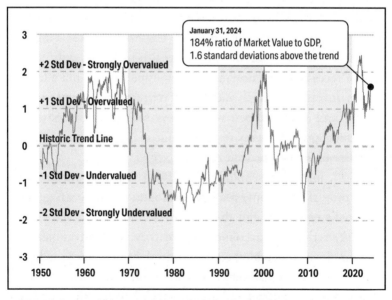

FIG. 3.1 Buffet Indictor: Standard deviations from the historic trend line of the stock market versus US GDP. *www.CurrentMarketValuation.com. Reproduced with permission.*

that their growth in value is simply outpacing the rest of the economy. But it could also mean that stocks are overvalued and a correction is a possibility on the horizon, or that we will implement unsustainable policies to try to prevent a correction.

In early 2024, the indicator was at 184 percent, meaning the value of the stock market was almost double GDP in terms of historical trends. Perhaps companies are innovating and outpacing GDP because of new products or more efficient processes, but we have seen persistent inflation over the past few years simply because companies can raise prices as they wish and because of the pressure from shareholders to maximize stock prices.

Wealth inequality

An overvalued stock market would be less problematic if it represented a larger percentage of the economy. More than half of US households now have at least some money invested in the stock market, which is good. The stock market is highly volatile and risky for short-term wealth-building, with inevitable recessions and downturns from time to time, but a long-term investment in an individual retirement account (IRA) is far and away the best way to save for retirement. Savings accounts provide paltry returns, while many IRAs have a long history of 7 to 10 percent returns over time.

Still, many households can't afford such investments or can only afford to invest a small amount. A family struggling to make ends meet but that has a few thousand dollars in a 401(k) retirement account because they took advantage of an employer's matching contribution does not care how high or low the stock market goes. Those households are decades away from retirement and are only trying to pay the monthly bills. They would be better off earning a living wage from their employers now and letting their 401(k)s grow a little slower because the employer spent more profit on wages than on buying back shares of company stock to increase returns for shareholders (more on this below).

As the stock market's value outpaces GDP, so does the percentage of stocks owned by the most wealthy. The top 10 percent of American households own 93 percent of the stocks, while the top 1 percent owns 53 percent.[3] In other words, though over half of US adults own stock, most of the worth is in the hands of a tiny portion of the population. The supremacy of the stock market has become a measure of how well the wealthy are doing, not how well the economy is doing. Yet whenever the stock market's value dips by a percentage point, perhaps because workers went on strike to demand higher wages, we hear about how the economy might be in trouble.

The other major contributing factor to wealth inequality is real estate.[4] As wealth concentrates, those households have more cash to invest in assets. Much of that wealth is invested in stocks, but a lot is also invested in commercial or residential real estate. As housing prices increase, this benefits the owners while preventing renters from having enough disposable income to pay down student loans or save a down payment to buy their own homes.

Stock buybacks

Stock buybacks are precisely what they sound like. Corporations buy their own shares, thereby reducing the total number of shares available, which drives up the price of the remaining shares. This is especially lucrative for executives of those corporations, who are often rewarded with shares as part of their compensation package. Buybacks were illegal before the Reagan-era process of deregulation, which sought to reduce government regulation and oversight to stimulate economic growth. They were considered stock manipulation for the benefit of the wealthy over workers. Reasonable parties might disagree, but I advocate that buybacks should be made illegal again. In general, corporations need more incentives to prioritize long-term growth over risky short-term gains.

The 2017 Republican tax cuts best illustrate how this practice is problematic. That legislation cut the corporate tax rate from 35 percent to 21 percent, freeing up more capital for companies. Many economists and activists hoped this cut would come with conditions like putting that money toward wages or innovation, but there were no stipulations. As a result, most of the freed-up capital went toward stock buybacks, inflating the stock market's value and dramatically increasing the national deficit and debt.[5] Since it is primarily the wealthy who own stocks, they are the ones who benefit the most while most of the country deals with the impact of rising national debt or reduced services and infrastructure.

Lowered tax rates for the wealthiest

No one particularly likes paying taxes, but much of the United States' ability to build infrastructure and pay for education and social safety nets during the middle of the twentieth century came from appropriately taxing the wealthiest households. For decades, tax rates for the wealthiest brackets have been trending downward. There is undoubtedly some good from that—freed-up capital can be used to create jobs and fund innovation. But much of that freed-up wealth has been spent buying up stocks and real estate, which is reflected in the increased percentage of the stock market owned by the wealthiest.

The issue of taxes and respective tax rates is surprisingly complex. For one, there is a legitimate argument about tax rates compared to taxes paid. Tax rates can be offset by tax exemptions, and the value of those exemptions has also changed frequently. When the highest tax rate was 90 percent, were exemptions to reduce taxes also higher? We tax income at one rate and capital gains (the sale of stocks, for instance) at a lower rate, and we do not tax wealth at all.

We also tend to misunderstand how tax brackets work, because only the income that exceeds the previous bracket gets taxed at the higher rate. If the tax rate is 20 percent up to $150,000 of annual income and 30 percent for income above that, only income you earn over $150,000 is taxed at the higher rate. If you earn $151,000, you might technically fall into the higher tax bracket, but it only slightly affects your taxes owed. This nuance can often be overlooked among people who are hesitant to support tax reform.

All that to say, tax rates are only one component of a more complex conversation. I suggest that the better strategy is to look at outcomes. The federal debt is increasing, national needs such as infrastructure and education are underfunded, and wealth inequality is increasing substantially. Perhaps taxes need to increase for everyone, not just the wealthy, or perhaps we need better enforcement of our existing tax laws through a fully funded and equipped Internal Revenue Service. Our tax

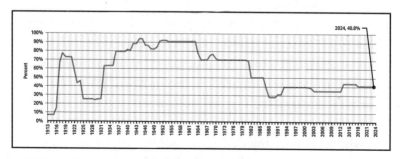

FIG. 3.2 Top US federal tax rates, 1913–2024. *Bradford Tax Institute.*

policies and processes will require more thoughtful consideration. But the outcomes are telling us that the wealthy are not paying their fair share.

Stagnant wages and inflation

Before the pandemic, real wages adjusted for inflation had remained stagnant for decades.[6] Inflation is tricky. In general, as the economy grows, the costs of living increases. When income increases, landlords know you can afford more rent, corporations know you can afford to pay more for goods and services, and you have more disposable income to spend, so the prices of other things go up. Those companies also must increase their employees' wages and pay more for goods and services, which influences what they charge. But inflation is not experienced uniformly.

There are many ways to calculate inflation, but the most common is the Consumer Price Index, which tracks the average price of a "basket of goods," including food, clothing, housing, fuel, transportation, and healthcare. Some things like televisions and calculators have gotten much more affordable. Of course, you may have noticed that the cost of certain goods have increased much faster. Healthcare, personal transportation, and housing have increased in price far faster than wages. My wife and I recently celebrated the end of buying diapers. We were always able to buy diapers in bulk, but I paid attention to the cost per diaper each time I bought an enormous box of them. The per diaper cost increased dramatically since my first child was born nearly a decade ago. Each time a diaper needed changing, I would think about a couple quarters going out the window. It . . . added up.

The years since the COVID-19 pandemic have been a constant fight between workers and inflation, with workers finally having negotiating power in a tight labor market. Much of the inflation over the past couple of years is a result of "greedflation," or when companies use increases in operating costs to justify raising the prices of goods and services far above those

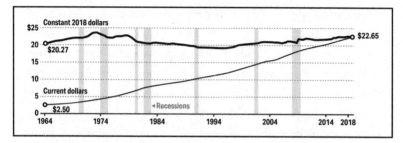

FIG. 3.3 "Americans' paychecks are bigger than 40 years ago, but their purchasing power has hardly budged." Hourly wages can be seen in current dollars versus 2018 dollars, 1964–2018. The "constant 2018 dollars" line shows the average wage based on the cost of living in 2018. Wages have increased, but it does not feel like they have increased. Further, this data reflects an average hourly wage. Since wages have disproportionately increased at the top of the scale, for the average wage to remain the same means those on the lower end of the pay scale have likely fallen behind in purchasing power. *Pew Research Center. Reproduced with permission.*

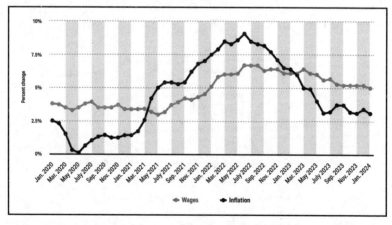

FIG. 3.4 Difference between the inflation rate and growth of wages in the United States, January 2020–January 2024. When wages were increasing at the fastest rates, inflation increased even faster. Even when inflation cooled to closer to 2.5 percent in mid-2023, it was still compounding growth on top of the prior years of 6 to 7 percent inflation. *Bureau of Labor Statistics; Federal Reserve Bank of Atlanta; US Census Bureau, February 2024. Chart by Statista. Reproduced with permission.*

costs—which is why so many companies have complained about having to increase worker wages while also posting record-breaking quarterly profits.[7] Essentially, for every $1 increase in the actual cost of wages and goods, companies raised their goods and services by about $2.

Meanwhile, workers know they are underpaid relative to their value. Between 1979 and 2020, workers' wages grew by 17.5 percent while productivity grew by 61.8 percent.[8] More substantial wage growth occurred among lower-wage jobs in 2022 and 2023, but much of that was due to increases in minimum wages in certain states.[9] The federal minimum wage continues to be stubbornly low. I care far more about living wage jobs than the minimum wage, but a reasonable minimum wage is critical for many households trying to become stable after a traumatic event or chronic poverty.

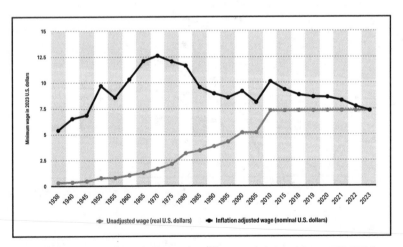

FIG. 3.5 Real and nominal value of the federal minimum wage in the United States, 1938–2023 (in 2023 US dollars). The actual minimum wage represented by the lower line has increased, but the value of the minimum wage based on the cost of living each year has remained stagnant and fallen in recent years. *US Department of Labor; Bureau of Labor Statistics, April 2023. Chart by Statista. Reproduced with permission.*

Limitless lobbying

Corporate lobbying reinforces and enhances a system that serves executives and shareholders better than workers and most households. This lobbying takes the form of corporations hiring individuals or firms to send professionals to communicate with lawmakers, help write policy, or donate to campaigns to influence policy decisions. Spending on lobbying has increased substantially over the years, reaching a new high of $4.1 billion in 2022. The top ten lobbying clients included the National Association of Realtors, the US Chamber of Commerce, several healthcare and pharmaceutical groups, and Amazon and Meta.[10]

Lobbying is a legitimate part of a healthy democratic system. Lawmakers are not experts in every issue for which they must write policies. Elected officials are responsible to voters, but citizens cannot be content experts in every issue either. So industry professionals are often best positioned to discuss the benefits or potential unintended consequences of policy choices. Perhaps members of Congress are considering a tax on imports of a foreign product, like steel, to protect domestic steel providers. This might be in response to advice from lobbyists hired by the steel companies to argue for protecting domestic steel jobs. But then, another industry that is worried about the subsequent increase in the cost of steel, perhaps the real estate industry or vehicle manufacturers, hires lobbyists to argue against tariffs or at least a tax break for those industries to offset possible costs.

One challenge, of course, is there are fewer lobby dollars for vulnerable subsets of the population. As with many other themes in this book, the goal is balance. Lobbying has a role to play, but it has tipped way out of balance in favor of those who already disproportionately benefit from the economic and political systems.

Diminished unions

Labor unions are imperfect organizations, but they have always been one of the best tools for workers to collectively go toe-to-toe with executives and shareholders to ensure workers get their fair share of the value of their contribution to productivity. In the United States, if someone has a non-management job with great pay, benefits, and some measure of job security, they are almost certainly part of a union. A significant contributor to the wealth inequality and supremacy of the stock market is the decline in union membership and subsequent loss of negotiating power.[11]

Unions essentially have themselves to blame, because they spent much of the twentieth century keeping themselves White and male while the workforce diversified.[12] There has been a welcome resurgence of unionizing in recent years, with employers desperately fighting back, but there is a long way to go to make up lost ground.

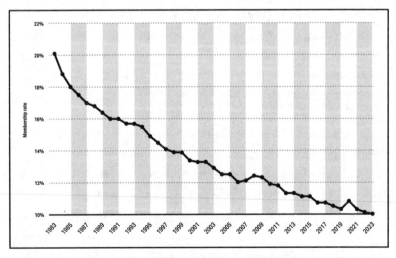

FIG. 3.6 Rate of union membership of employees in the United States, 1983–2022. *Bureau of Labor Statistics. Chart by Statista. Reproduced with permission.*

Unrestricted campaign finance

In 2010, while wealth inequality surged and worker power declined, the 5–4 Supreme Court decision in *Citizens United v. Federal Election Commission* unleashed the wealthy to invest in accelerating these trends. The ruling declared that restricting "independent political spending" violated the First Amendment.

Today, we generally take for granted that super PACs (political action committees) exist and fund candidates who will vote to support the interests of wealthy benefactors, but they are a relatively new creation. *Citizens United* allowed billions of dollars of dark money—"dark" because the donors' identities may remain hidden—to be funneled through super PACs that spend those funds to support certain candidates and attack others. Not surprisingly, many super PACs favor more tax cuts and deregulation.[13] As we have seen in recent decades, excessive tax cuts and deregulation lead to greater wealth inequality, an increased sense of entitlement among the wealthy for even more, and increased scarcity for working families.

Rising federal spending and debt

Meanwhile, we are in a "rock and a hard place" dynamic with federal spending. There is much hand-wringing about the national debt and spending. The current national debt is more than $34 trillion. The interest on that debt will continue to eat up more of the federal budget as interest rates climb. However, we do not look at actual spending, which reveals a problem about how to get from a deficit to a surplus so that we might pay that debt down at some point.

Achieving a budget surplus requires cutting spending and increasing income—in this case, taxes. We've already talked about how we've cut taxes dramatically for corporations and the wealthy. Some people believe the benefits of these cuts will outweigh the consequences over time. The nonpartisan Congressional Budget Office, however, regularly affirms that the combination of tax cuts and increased spending on entitlement programs is leading to record debt levels.[14]

There are three main categories of federal spending: mandatory spending (which is dictated by laws rather than the annual budget process), discretionary spending (which is set by Congress each year), and interest payments on the national debt (which varies according to interest rates). Mandatory spending represents the lion's share of the budget, but it requires agreement on legislation to make changes. Therefore, the relatively smaller bucket of discretionary spending is vulnerable to politics and includes things like the military, education, transportation, and law enforcement.

A significant percentage of federal spending is on entitlement programs (Social Security, Medicare, Medicaid), which fall under mandatory spending. While mandatory spending isn't subject to annual budget reconciliation, it is still at the whims of the political process. Especially after the passage of the Affordable Care Act, Medicare spending has increased significantly as a percentage of the budget.[15] Social Security costs are also increasing as life expectancy increases and smaller generations of workers replace those who are retiring. However, many seniors heavily rely on Social Security benefits to meet their needs.[16] Where are cuts to be made, and who will pay for it?

The solution is simple on paper: We either raise taxes, cut spending, which will cause harm wherever we do it, or start getting better at compromise and writing legislation to make our systems work more efficiently, which is very difficult in today's political environment. But the only other option is to

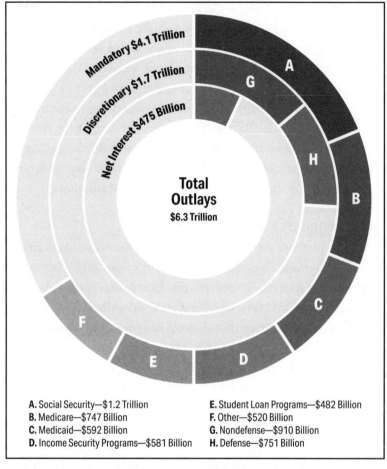

FIG. 3.7 Total outlays in the 2022 federal budget. [GL: Source] Dan Ready, Jorge Salazar, and Caitlin Verboon, *The Federal Budget in Fiscal Year 2022: An Infographic* (Congressional Budget Office, March 2023).

do what we are doing now: keep cutting taxes, increase spending, avoid hard policy conversations, and let the debt keep building until something breaks.

This environment, where all the options are hard and someone will be mad no matter what you do or don't do, is ripe for idolatry. When we feel like something isn't working or isn't sustainable, we each worry we'll be the one left without a chair when the music stops. We might worry someone else is taking advantage of the system at our expense. We become vulnerable to simple narratives about minority groups, people with privilege or wealth, or opposing political representatives. Hence, language and symbols have become rampant in clouding that decision. In addition to the math and the policies, we need to be clear about the language preventing us from reaching a consensus about the problems and solutions.

EXAMINING OUR GOLDEN IDOLS

As we saw from the interaction between Paul and Samantha, their values and language to articulate values differ in ways they do not necessarily understand. That makes them vulnerable to division and fear, which makes them vulnerable to idols. The greed outlined in this chapter fuels wealthy households to support divisiveness to keep the spotlight off them. Make sure poor White people, poor Black people, seniors, and other vulnerable groups blame each other for their woes instead of noticing that the United States had 715 billionaires in 2023, up from 442 in 2013, which was already way too many.[17]

The Israelites under Aaron turned to a physical golden idol. Sometimes the idols we turn to are ideas or symbols. Some of the language we use or allegiances we celebrate point to secondary masters that can become idols in moments of fear or anger if we are not careful. There are some vulnerable ideas and terms that currently threaten to divide us—but if turned on their heads, I think they can lead to increased empathy and unity. In considering a few of these potential golden idols, I hope we can become better prepared to listen rather than judge.

Capitalism versus neoliberalism

Economic peacemaking requires breaking away from the simplistic narrative of capitalism and socialism as two ends of a spectrum, one good and one bad, which defines our relationship with money and the economy. This simplistic narrative is often represented as the free market versus the oppressive state. In reality, capitalism and the free market system are made possible by a functioning democratic state. In the United States, the classifications of corporations are created and defined by our government. We then depend on the government to maintain a system in which monopolies cannot rise so far above their competitors that they can bully or buy out everyone, raise prices, and reduce the quality of products and services.

Healthy capitalism requires a healthy democracy that creates an environment that rewards competition and innovation with the potential for wealth. Thriving capitalism means strong unions ensuring wealth is distributed fairly to workers, not just executives and shareholders. When we hear capitalism being thrown about as the only economic system that Christians can support since the alternative is evil socialism, we are unwittingly committing ourselves to an idol. For about forty years now, the United States has emphasized deregulation, tax cuts, removing the social safety net, and demolishing unions.[18] We thought the government was the enemy, so we reduced the role of government in the economy and turned more power and wealth over to corporations. This is a specific, radical version of capitalism called neoliberalism.

Unfortunately, neoliberal economics (aka "trickle-down economics") is terrible for peacemaking. Greed is never satisfied, so when corporations accumulate wealth, their shareholders feel entitled to even more. So we deregulate, we cut taxes. Wages are suppressed, benefits are cut, and jobs are moved overseas or replaced with technology. The government also does not take in as much money in taxes, so it reduces spending on education and infrastructure. The burden of neo-liberalism falls heavily on workers and low-income communities. People who already have wealth in the stock market or real estate accumulate unfathomable wealth, and the frustration starts to boil over. People who can't find good jobs to afford housing and food start turning to crime and drugs. The government builds more prisons, and we start down the road away from peacemaking toward merely peacekeeping, which does not work.

Capitalism versus socialism

The simplistic narrative goes both ways. Younger generations are often vulnerable to the argument that free markets are evil and that we should turn to socialism so that the government will tax those greedy corporations and turn that wealth over to the people. I believe that this generational divide is an opportunity for building empathy. Older generations that remember the Cold War with the USSR had a very different relationship to socialism. Back then, *socialism* was used interchangeably with *communism*. It was the United States' democratic free market versus the Soviet communist state-managed economy. The Soviets had a lower quality of life; the government that was supposed to be for the people kept many people in poverty to enrich the powerful, and then that whole system crumbled.

After the fall of the Soviet Union, the United States experienced a decade of being the dominant world superpower and enjoyed significant economic growth and prosperity. The Cold War had been a lifelong, stressful, sometimes terrifying ordeal. That visceral reaction to the word *socialism* will not go away for the generations who experienced that. The rest of us can work to understand that perspective and maybe be more careful with our terminology.

The opportunity is not to fight for a new definition of socialism but to reclaim the very idea of capitalism. Healthy capitalism will provide a robust social safety net and clear pathways to be rehired or retrained for a living wage job. The fear of being taken advantage of, which seems especially prevalent in a country like America, with its history of taking advantage of people, causes us to hesitate to use the carrot, and thus we rely on the stick. The stick is keeping households living paycheck to paycheck, making poverty and homelessness an ever-present danger. But the carrot of a living wage job is the most potent tool we have to minimize dependency.

One nuance is what younger generations often mean by socialism, which is democratic socialism, or a state that provides a robust social safety net within a free market system. Tax rates would be higher for the wealthy to pay for this social safety net, but not so much that it stifles the incentive to innovate or take risks, which happens in a communist system. This argument has some merit. Is it better to have more billionaires and many millions of increasingly angry and hopeless people working multiple jobs and still unable to meet basic needs, or to have fewer billionaires (but still many centimillionaires) and more people participating in a system that offers economic opportunity for average people? Those of us with a visceral reaction to the historical meaning of *socialism* can be proactive to empathize with younger generations and to understand what they are trying to communicate.

Wealth and prosperity

Mixing an idol with Christianity leads to diluted or perverted theology. A wholehearted belief in capitalism as God's economic system has led to a belief that God wants you to be (financially) wealthy, that accumulating wealth is a sign that you have earned God's favor, and that poverty means you are sinning or rejecting God in some way. In this understanding, wealth inequality shows who the good Christians are. This is a fundamental dynamic of the prosperity gospel, which rose to prominence in the 1980s with promises of financial blessing for being aligned with God's will. Within that theological framework, more wealth means more assurance that God is pleased with your spirituality.

We know the prosperity gospel is false because Jesus directly addressed it multiple times. He clearly understood this would be an enduring temptation. Jesus loved parables and metaphors, but when it came to money, he flat out said we cannot serve both God and money (Matthew 6:24). He told us to sell our possessions and give to the poor because our treasure is in heaven (Luke 12:32–34). He warned that it will be difficult for a rich person to enter the kingdom of God (Mark 10:24–25), and he warned against the deceitfulness of wealth (Matthew 13:18–24). Precisely what this means for each of us, how much we aspire to earn, and how much of that we will give we each must work out for ourselves. But we do know that following Jesus is not a path to earthly wealth.

Spiritualizing wealth creates a problem in that we don't have to think about the systems we participate in or scrutinize our behavior and assumptions. The problem with this blindness that comes from idol worship is that when peace becomes predictably more complex to make and violence or the threat of violence increases, we cannot question ourselves. We double down; we put even more faith in the idol; we demand even more tax cuts for the wealthy and corporations and more deregulation.

The "truth"

In the garden of Eden, the serpent said to Eve, "You will not certainly die. . . For God knows that when you eat from [the tree in the middle of the garden] your eyes will be opened, and you will be like God, knowing good and evil" (Genesis 3:4–5). In part, we want to be like God, or at least to fashion our own gods we can influence and control. But we also want insider knowledge. We want to know good and evil. We want to be the ones who know what is true.

Alongside our weakness to turn to an idol when times get tough or we are hurt or scared, we add the rise of politicized cable news and social media that enhances disinformation and elevates anything that exploits our fears or trauma. That results in our current situation, where we respond to real problems by making those problems worse through more divisiveness and the threat of violence. When our truths become subjective, we become vulnerable to idolatry. We take a bite of the fruit and point at an immigrant, declaring it is true they took our job. Someone else takes a bite of the fruit and points at a billionaire, stating it is true that he and the system in which he generates wealth are evil. If a political leader or talking head says, "This Golden Charging Bull is the God who led you out of Egypt . . . now, let's have a feast to the Lord!," do we have the faith, maturity, and humility to repent and run in the other direction?

Counterintuitively, knowing we all are vulnerable to this lust for God's knowledge, and vulnerable to crafting idols that permit us to live according to our subjective truths, provides a solution and a way forward. This is Christianity 101: "You, therefore, have no excuse, you who pass judgment on someone else, for at whatever point you judge another, you are condemning yourself, because you who pass judgment do the same things" (Romans 2:1). Rather than turning over every rock and kicking in every door looking for idols that will give us that "Aha!" moment so many of us long for, we can embrace the foundational tenet of Christianity that we are all sinners, repent for our history of greed and our ongoing participation in a system based on greed, and turn our attention to the planks in our own eyes before we start concerning ourselves with the specks in our neighbors'.

DISCUSSION QUESTIONS

1. Do you know a Paul or Samantha? In what ways might you be vulnerable to a similar situation yourself?
2. How do larger-scale economic trends reflect what is happening in your community?
3. What is something you have thought related to economic peacemaking that you suspect might be an overly simplistic narrative or is a result of using a different language than others?

THE PLANKS IN OUR EYES

To be a poor man is hard, but to be a poor race in a land of dollars is the very bottom of hardships.
—W. E. B. Du Bois, *The Souls of Black Folks*

I have no idea what I'm doing, but I know I'm doing it really, really well.
—Andy Dwyer, in *Parks and Recreation*

Recently, the Christian university I attended twenty years earlier nearly closed and ended up being abosrbed by another university. I had never logged on to the alumni page before, but I finally did so to express my sadness as well as thankfulness for the transformational experience I had there. What I found was rage and rejoicing because the university had, apparently, strayed from its strict adherence to biblical values and was experiencing God's punishment.

The narrative was that the university had spent too much time talking about diversity, equity, empathy, and community building and too little time judging the world for perceived sexual sin. Granted, this alumni group had become small. Like other online spaces, this virtual community allowed for outrage to be magnified, and it appeared to cause many other alumni to disconnect. Unfortunately, this has the unintended consequence of making the angry minority even more embittered because they feel unheard and start breaking things and causing division wherever they can. Then, for outsiders paying attention, that minority starts to represent the whole.

The world is paying attention to Christians to see whether our behavior matches our words, to see whether we *really* believe this or whether we merely *say* we believe it. They often do not see the majority of us quietly loving our neighbors and demonstrating the fruits of the Spirit. Even those of us quietly serving and loving our neighbors can overlook one another, which can let that minority affect our identities as well.

Jesus also dealt with the angry minority religious elite, who wanted to accuse him of not adhering to God's Law so that they could continue living in hypocrisy. One of the most beautiful and gut-wrenching biblical stories is a simple one from John 8. Jesus was teaching at the temple courts when the teachers of the law and the Pharisees brought him the woman caught in adultery. They say, "Teacher, this woman was caught in the act of adultery. In the Law Moses commanded us to stone such women. Now what do you say?" The text reports, "They were using this question as a trap, in order to have a basis for accusing him" (vv. 4–6). Jesus bends down, starts to write in the sand, stands up, and says those iconic words: "Let any one of you who is without sin be the first to throw a stone at her" (v. 7). Then he stoops down again and keeps writing. The people in the crowd leave one at a time until only the woman remains. Jesus tells the woman he does not condemn her, but he also commands her to leave her life of sin.

What Jesus might have written in the sand is debated, but in the way one debates how good an NFL draft was. We're not supposed to know; we're supposed to wonder. Was he writing the names of each person present, the names of people with whom each of the accusers had committed adultery or other laws of Moses they had each broken? The fact that they left one by one tells me it was intimate and shocking. The point is clear: Do not judge, because you are a sinner, too. Only Jesus has the authority to judge, and even he is uninterested. He did instruct the woman to stop sinning, but only after he had established that he loved her and was not interested in judging her for the sake of having someone to judge.

When I dwell on this story, another instruction from Jesus bubbles to mind. "Do not judge, or you too will be judged," Jesus says in the Beatitudes.

> For in the same way you judge others, you will be judged, and with the measure you use, it will be measured to you.
>
> Why do you look at the speck of sawdust in your brother's eye and pay no attention to the plank in your own eye? How can you say to your brother, 'Let me take the speck out of your eye,' when all the time there is a plank in your own eye? You hypocrite, first take the plank out of your own eye, and then you will see clearly to remove the speck from your brother's eye. (Matthew 7:1–5)

We could keep going. Luke 6 repeats Jesus' instruction. In his letter to the Romans, Paul writes about not judging others (Romans 14). James writes about it in the fourth chapter of his letter.

So as I walk through the world wanting to live with morality and take up my cross and die to myself daily, I also ask, "What are the planks in my eyes? And if I brought the woman caught in adultery before Jesus to be stoned, what would he write in the sand about me?" Through that lens, how do I act as a peacemaker with integrity?

It's an odd time to be a Christian in a leadership position. I am an elder with my local church, I teach at a private Christian university, and I am an unapologetic Christian out in the world engaging with both conservative and progressive contexts. Unfortunately, this is a time when Christians in leadership positions are frequently asked what they think about homosexuality, same-sex marriage, and so on. In general, I am uninterested in imposing the Bible on the broader culture to legislate behavior. Even if I were, Jesus' instruction about planks and his actions of drawing in the sand communicate that motives and history matter. And I believe that the trauma inflicted on the LGBTQIA+ community, often by professing Christians, supersedes the theological concerns some people may have.

Set aside for a moment the arguments about what the Bible says about sexuality and what precisely Paul is referring to when he calls out "men who have sex with men" in 1 Corinthians 6:9, which is couched in a section about lawsuits among believers. After many "shame on you" statements, Paul writes:

> The very fact that you have lawsuits among you means you have been completely defeated already. Why not rather be wronged? Why not rather be cheated? Instead, you yourselves cheat and do wrong, and you do this to your brothers and sisters. Or do you not know that wrongdoers will not inherit the kingdom of God? Do not be deceived: Neither the sexually immoral nor idolaters nor adulterers nor men who have sex with men nor thieves nor the greedy nor drunkards nor slanderers nor swindlers will inherit the kingdom of God. And that is what some of you were. But you were washed, you were sanctified, you were justified in the name of the Lord Jesus Christ and by the Spirit of our God. (1 Corinthians 6:7–11)

Let's consider another Pauline passage often used to describe why God is so concerned about issues of sexuality identity. In 1 Timothy 1, Paul writes:

> The goal of this command is love, which comes from a pure heart and a good conscience and a sincere faith. Some have departed from these and have turned to meaningless talk. They want to be teachers of the law, but they do not know what they are talking about or what they so confidently affirm.
>
> We know that the law is good if one uses it properly. We also know that the law is made not for the righteous but for lawbreakers and rebels, the ungodly and sinful, the unholy and irreligious, for those who kill their fathers or mothers, for murderers, for the sexually immoral, for those practicing homosexuality, for slave traders and liars and perjurers—and for whatever else is contrary to the sound doctrine that conforms to the gospel concerning the glory of the blessed God, which he entrusted to me. (1 Timothy 1:5–11)

This is not *the* definitive list of sins. Part of what Paul identifies in 1 Timothy is that there isn't a list. Love is the law. If it is loving God and loving your neighbor, it is good. If it is anything else, it is nothing, and it is quite possibly sin.

Even though these two passages are not definitive lists of sinful behaviors, I feel some fingers pointed my way. I spy some planks I need to pay attention to. Not only the sexually immoral, but idolaters will not enter the kingdom of heaven! Not just those practicing homosexuality, but drunkards, slanderers, and liars! How many Christians judge others for sexuality but themselves struggle with unhealthy consumption? Or slander politicians they don't like? Or choose to believe lies and idolize liars?

And the greedy will not inherit the kingdom of God.

MISSING THE PLANKS

I have always enjoyed running but keep dealing with injuries as I enter middle age. Last year, I finally transitioned from running to swimming, which has been spectacular. However, there is a scarcity of swimming. You can run pretty much anywhere, and gyms all over the place have cardio equipment. Swimming lanes can be hard to find. I experimented, awkwardly, at a newer community center in my neighborhood with many swim lanes. It was great at first, but it became very stressful as I started to gain confidence and wanted to swim more frequently.

Over the past few years, it's been challenging to fill the minimum wage part-time lifeguarding positions. This meant the pool was often closed. There were only a few swim sessions during the week. This translated into packed lanes with swimmers doubling up and lines of swimmers waiting to take their turn. I started looking for alternatives. I found a private fitness center farther away with a lap pool open all day.

A few weeks after I started swimming there, a leak formed in the ceiling, and the pool shut down for over a month of repairs. I tried running in the meantime and reinjured myself, so when the pool finally reopened, I eagerly returned. A few weeks later, I was swimming laps and noticed what looked like ripples. On no, not another leak, I worried. A few days later, I was swimming again and saw more ripples in the same spot, then again a few days later. Dejected and a little salty, I mentioned to the staff person at the front on my way out that I thought there might be another leak. To my surprise, he said they had been hearing that a lot. It wasn't a leak in the roof; new jets were installed while the pool was shut down. They upgraded the system to make the pool a few degrees warmer. It turns out there had been many complaints about the cold temperature for a long time. It was a whole thing. During the shutdown, they finally decided to fix this problem that I did not know even existed.

Sure enough, the next time I went swimming, I put my hand down as I passed the jets and could feel the upward force of the water. I noticed that the water felt a bit warmer, something I had not paid attention to before, being lost in my world and distracted by the day's thoughts as I went through the motions.

This exceedingly frivolous example demonstrates the need for curiosity as we pass through the world. I interpreted the signs of what was happening only through the narrow scope of my recent history. I never asked myself whether something else could be going on. I only knew about the scarcity of swim lanes, the propensity for that availability to be taken away or restricted at a moment's notice, and the apparent ever-present risk of ceiling leaks. Meanwhile, I was utterly oblivious to the conversation and history around water temperature, but it did affect my experience.

Even at that moment, I wondered how often I do this. How frequently do I assume I know what's happening in some context when, in reality, the truth is far more nuanced, complex, and concealed? How much more would I learn, and how much more effective could I be, if I go through the world assuming there is much I do not know and curious to uncover some of it? I would lose a false sense of control over my environment and time spent judging others. That sounds like a win-win.

I DON'T KNOW

Many of us struggle to embrace the words "I don't know." I don't know (!) where this comes from, at least not entirely.

Perhaps it results from our tendency to over-spiritualize our lives. If we "pray on" something, our subsequent actions must be God's will. If we get a feeling about something, the Holy Spirit must tell us whether something is good or evil. This puts us in a position to never feel out of control. We know, we see, we're right. Even if I don't "know" know, I feel like I know. I certainly don't not know.

An unintended result of over-spiritualizing our lives is redefining what assurance means. The Bible talks about assurance as hope and confidence that this will all be worth it and that God's love will prevail. It does not indicate that believers will have unshakeable self-confidence about their salvation. We should not expect an assurance that displaces all doubt. "Faith is confidence in what we hope for and assurance about what we do not see," says Hebrews 11:1.

In the apostle Paul's first letter to the Corinthians, he names that speaking in tongues, prophesies, and works are nothing without love. "For now we see only a reflection as in a mirror; then we shall see face to face. Now I know in part; then I shall know fully, even as I am fully known. And now, these three remain: faith, hope and love. But the greatest of these is love" (1 Corinthians 13:12–13). I take a lot of comfort from these words. I take even more comfort a couple of chapters later when Paul writes, "I face death every day . . . if the dead are not raised, 'Let us eat and drink, for tomorrow we die'" (15:31–32). Even Paul says of himself, essentially, I'd better be right because if I'm wrong, all this would have been a massive waste of time. He has some doubts, but he has faith, hope, and love.

These passages encourage me to embrace "I don't know." No one fully understands their context or the whole truth about anything. And anyone who is being honest understands that no one else knows. Anyone who claims to know unequivocally loses credibility. Anyone who demonstrates faith, hope, and love has my allegiance.

From the information I can gather and the signs I can perceive in my context, I think I know people need living wage jobs if we are going to maintain and enhance peace in our communities and our country. But what do I not know that I do not understand?

I DIDN'T KNOW

My first job in the social service sector was with a Catholic nonprofit organization engaged in refugee resettlement. My job was to drive around the city collecting donations in a big van and then use those donations to furnish apartments for arriving refugee families. I also got to help orient them to their new homes and was responsible for a warehouse where all the donations were kept. I organized all the donated clothing and hung it up so that I could bring refugee families through and let them pick out new clothing for themselves. It was an excellent opportunity to serve and love families that had survived traumatic experiences, sometimes for many years before they qualified for resettlement.

Occasionally, I was asked to help with other events. I was invited to assist with an event at an apartment complex where many refugee families who had all come from the same encampment were placed. A strong community had formed there, and they supported newer arrivals. Because there would be a series of activities for children at the complex, I went into the warehouse and pulled out a large box of inflatable toys that had been donated, including dozens of inflatable balls, bats, plastic frisbees, and other items. I put the box in the van and drove to the complex. When the event started, and all the children were present, I pulled out the box and began distributing items. I imagined we would all play, and there would be bats and inflatable balls everywhere. But each child grabbed as many items as possible, ran into their respective apartments, and returned empty-handed. No one played with any of the toys I had brought.

To my great shame, I responded with judgment in my heart at that time. What a lack of appreciation! Why ruin this generosity with selfishness and hoarding so we miss out on an opportunity to play together? After many years of failing and shameful judgment that eventually led to more empathy and insight, I now understand. Those children had grown up with nothing. They fought over access to necessities such as food, water, and shelter. There was never enough for everyone. You had to battle to get anything, and then you would have to fight to keep it. I grew up in relative abundance. My family was middle-class, and there were shelves of toys and food everywhere. As a young man, I didn't understand how those differences would manifest in everyday behavior. More importantly, I had no idea I didn't know that I didn't know that. Assuming I knew led to judgment and turned me toward bitterness.

Today, I am more disciplined and practiced to assume that there is a dynamic at play I do not understand and to commit to loving my neighbor. I have a long way to go, but I try to default to curiosity rather than judgment. That feels to me like Christianity, like what Jesus would do in this complex world. I pray it gets me a little further away from bringing the woman caught in adultery to Jesus to be stoned and a little closer to telling her she is not condemned, but for both of us to stop sinning.

GREEDIOCY

The elephant in the room is the truth that greed is the fundamental sin of White American Christianity. I sometimes wonder, do we really not know it is there? Do we know but try to offset this guilt by fervently holding people accountable for other behaviors? I am not sure, but there can be no peace-making without repentance and reconciliation for the many sins we are responsible for out of greed. We have no business judging anyone for anything until we acknowledge and repair this damage. These sins weren't committed only by White people or only by Christians, but White American Christianity often condoned, justified, or benefited from them.

The US government committed and permitted genocide and land theft against Native Americans. The nation tolerated slavery because it generated so much wealth. Then, after a civil war in which 620,000 people died that ended with offi-cially abolishing slavery, our nation reneged on its economic peacemaking promises to its Black citizens. In 1865, General William Tecumseh Sherman issued an order to provide "forty acres and a mule" to freed slaves as a peaceful transition to an integrated country. When Andrew Johnson assumed the presidency after Abraham Lincoln was assassinated, Johnson overturned Sherman's directive. This was one of many political efforts to undercut and eventually overthrow Reconstruction, which sought to reunite the nation and advance equality for African Americans.

A few decades later, Jim Crow policies sought to maintain the economic benefits of slavery while technically not permit-ting it. Non-White households were prevented from attaining assets such as homes that would become mechanisms for inter-generational wealth that would set stable families apart from unstable ones. Then, when Black Americans finally achieved significant civil rights legislation victories in the 1960s, poli-cies and politicians conveniently started decimating the social safety net. The derogatory term "welfare queen" described an imagined Black woman with no job, living large off of government programs. This exaggerated stereotype was used to affirm suspicions of all Black welfare recipients, and the idea was so detestable that White Americans reacted by reducing the social safety net and welfare system.[1] Throughout US history, Black and Brown immigrants have been welcomed in to work for very little money, then condemned and forced out when others feared they might compete for their jobs. And still today, women are chronically underpaid, or not compensated at all.

In today's economy, we care a whole lot about the value of the stock market, which does not reflect the economic situation or opportunity for most households. We suppress wages, lay off workers, cut benefits, cut hours for hourly workers, and demand more hours from salaried workers. Then we dare to complain about crime, fatigue, and hopelessness, which were always going to result from these decisions. It is idolatry. It is greed. It is greed that hurts even the very people complaining about the consequences of greed. Greediocy.

I imagine Jesus would write the name of a slave-trading ancestor in the sand, or the member of a Native tribe who was killed for the land on which my house is built, or the names of the children who mined the materials for my phone.[2]

IGNORING OUR DEBTS

On a macro scale, this can be overwhelming. The planks of greediocy are so embedded in our eyes it can feel like a better strategy to just try to ignore or justify them. Just claim to be color-blind and give some money to charity. Let's be too busy being mad about other issues to worry about it.

I know the feeling of not wanting to pay any attention to the debts you owe. My first job out of college was driving a garbage truck, and part of my route included yard debris pickups, which slowed down during the winter months. That job was hourly, so slower routes meant less money. The head gasket blew on my car when things were already lean in the middle of winter. I took it to a mechanic, and the cost maxed out my credit card. Then someone at the repair shop cracked my windshield so severely that I could not see out of it, and they refused to accept responsibility, assuring me this was how they received it. I sold some of my few possessions and borrowed some cash to get the windshield fixed so I could drive to work.

After the next lean paycheck, I knew I needed to put some of that toward paying down my accumulated debt. Internet access was limited then, and calling the bank to get an update was more common. I remember reaching to pick up that phone many times, only to find something else to do. What was the point? It would only be bad news, and my paltry paycheck would only be a drop in the bucket. The energy required to face the problem was more significant than the impact I could have trying to solve the problem.

Later in life, being in the volatile nonprofit world, I was laid off a few months after buying a house. Our first child was a toddler, and my wife was pregnant with our second, so she could not seek work at that time. The pressure and stress were immense. Those were brutal months getting through that experience and finding stability again. After getting through that situation, I remember logging on to my credit card account, seeing my debt situation, and finding other things to do. I was exhausted from surviving; how would I muster the energy to start thinking about the future again and begin the long process of repaying the debts I had accumulated just trying to get through hard times?

I was a workforce development case manager during the Great Recession in the late 2000s. At that time, I met with many people enrolling in college, partly to retrain themselves for jobs that were in demand and partly to get access to student loans to pay the bills as they survived those rough times. A decade later, I was a financial coach meeting with people who had accumulated significant school debt during the Great Recession. They had worked themselves back to stability, but they knew those loans were looming and accumulating interest. They wanted to pretend that debt wasn't there. They were better off than during the recession, but were in no way wealthy or in a place to quickly pay those debts. The thought was exhausting. I could relate.

SOCIAL JUSTICE AND PEACEMAKING

Owning up to the debts we have incurred is daunting. What should the expectations be for households that are relatively well off? Give away homes and donate the entirety of paychecks to struggling households, impoverishing their own children along the way? No, but Christians are called to generosity and empathy. And in the long run, those in the next generations will also benefit by living in more peaceful communities with better economic opportunities. In the same way that adopting "color blindness" after creating severe disparity along racial lines will not cure racism, making peace is not achievable without acknowledging the harm and hypocrisy of greed. And in my experience, the communities who have experienced this harm do not demand that White people switch places, with White people now subjugating themselves. Most communities are thirsty for reconciliation and pragmatic solutions. They are often quick to forgive and want to partner to build more peaceful communities and ensure economic opportunities for everyone.

This is why I have largely purged my vocabulary of "social justice." I object not to social justice per se but rather to simplistic narratives about social justice. These narratives have taken on a connotation of thinking about reconciliation for the past and establishing equity today, but they often do not incorporate current challenges and future threats that may hold back more privileged stakeholders, even those who want to generously engage in this work. A simplistic social justice lens often leads to calls for wealth transfer without establishing systems that work for everyone. That is how we call for the end of coal jobs in West Virginia and new jobs in sustainable energy elsewhere in the country without addressing what the former coal workers and their children will do for a living.

That said, community economic development without a social justice lens is ineffective. That is how we end up having goals for historically marginalized communities that those communities reject. Many social service initiatives aspire to help families afford the cheapest two-bedroom apartments in their communities, but those are often unsafe and in places with limited economic opportunities. Those families want to overcome the disparity in intergenerational wealth-building, attain a mortgage, pay off that asset in their lifetimes, and have something to pass on to their children. Social service project managers and project funders often scoff at that goal if we do not think about the social injustice that has occurred. This is also why we still have programs that help people attain jobs that pay far less than most of us would accept for ourselves. Communities aspire to earn a living wage at a dignified job, and a social justice lens helps keep all the stakeholders focused on that goal.

Real peacemaking incorporates social justice, thinking about righting the wrongs of the past and investing in a peaceful and sustainable future. This is why I have replaced *social justice* with *peacemaking*: it is more comprehensive. This lens is how we think pragmatically and compassionately about all the many elements required for economic peacemaking: education, early childhood development, living wage jobs, voting, home ownership, supporting teachers, grocery stores, parks, libraries, infrastructure, and so on.

THINKING TACOMA

It is more feasible and productive to think about the planks in the eyes of our local communities and the individual relationships and conversations that might take place in pursuit of economic peacemaking than to identify concrete national or global strategies. My city of Tacoma contains a fascinating snapshot of many national dynamics that influence how we think about jobs and the economy today.

Native sovereignty

The Puyallup Tribe of Indians are located within and adjacent to the City of Tacoma. The territory of Washington was problematic from its start. Non-Native settlers began pouring into the region in the mid-nineteenth century. The Puyallup reservation was established when the US government pressured the tribes to authorize documents that signed away their lands and established three small reservations. The Treaty Wars of 1855 and 1856 occurred shortly thereafter. The Puyallup Tribe has consistently had to defend and protect itself from US government attempts to break up or dilute its tribal culture and land. This has been especially acute around fishing rights and the sustainability of Commencement Bay as the commercial industry continues to grow and pollute the waters.

In recent decades, the tribe has invested heavily in economic development initiatives. One of those initiatives is an enormous and ever-growing casino. This casino is next to one of Tacoma's lowest-income regions, so many residents work there, in no small part because it is one of few employers within walking distance. Gambling addiction is a significant barrier to helping lower-income households thrive and become self-sufficient.

The Puyallup Tribe also suffers from a high percentage of missing and murdered Indigenous women and people (MMIWP). So we have a community in close proximity, with historical distrust, an economy that is both entangled in and at odds with Tacoma's economy, and significant social and criminal factors that are poorly understood. Many well-intended peacemakers have intended to put hand to plow and get good work done only to find themselves judging the Puyallup Tribe for these casinos, unaware of the complex history and context that preceded them.

Immigrant exclusion and expulsion

The US government passed the shameful National Chinese Expulsion Act in 1882, and Tacoma followed suit in 1885 with its own Chinese expulsion. As early as the 1850s, the United States opened its borders and allowed Chinese immigrants to provide cheap labor and thus lower-cost goods and services. They also provided labor for the jobs that many White Americans did not want, such as working in the mines and building the railroad. An economic downturn caused the White residents to blame the Chinese workers for taking their jobs. In November 1885, a mob rounded up all the Chinese in the city and forced them out of town. Today, a reconciliation park on the waterfront reminds and warns us about the future. Still, many residents drive by the park every day, oblivious to the modern relevance of those lessons.

In recent years, awareness has increased regarding the internment of Japanese citizens during World War II. Residents of Tacoma were among those removed from their homes and placed in internment camps, and some had their homes or land taken from them during or after internment.[3] The camps themselves were not located in the city, but one of the assembly centers where residents were gathered for transport to the camps was located nearby.

As elsewhere in the United States, Tacoma has a problematic relationship with undocumented immigrants. Washington's large agricultural sector largely depends on this labor to maximize profits and keep the prices of apples and wine relatively low. These workers, many from Latin America, also help keep costs low for other products and services, including construction, kitchens, housekeeping, entry-level manufacturing, and home healthcare. Tacomans have immediate fears about the cost of undocumented households receiving services and getting access to education and healthcare, and longer-term anxiety that the second and third generations will grow up assimilated and compete for jobs. All of this manifests as a desire to simultaneously incentivize and exploit undocumented immigrant labor and then deport them. Sometimes it manifests as anti-immigrant violence.[4]

Many immigrant communities make up the diverse community Tacoma has become. Washington's relative proximity to Asia and thriving tech sector make it an attractive region for wealthy Asian households. Tacoma received a significant number of Vietnamese and Cambodian refugees in the 1970s after the fall of Saigon and the end of the Vietnam War. There is also a solid Nordic culture thanks to significant immigration from Scandinavian countries in the nineteenth and twentieth centuries.

One of the largest US Immigration and Customs Enforcement (ICE) detention facilities is in the Port of Tacoma, close to the Eastside of Tacoma, where many Hispanic households reside. A private corporation operates the 1,500-bed detention center. Many immigrants, but especially Spanish speakers, live in fear of being detained and deported and possibly separated from their families. Several churches and a nonprofit organization maintain a presence at the facility's entrance to offer services and comfort to traumatized families, as well as translation and legal services. However, there are regular hunger strikes due to conditions within the facility. It is not uncommon to meet with someone, often a woman, who is looking for a job because her husband was just deported and she has no other way of supporting their child. Returning to their home country is often not an option because of gang violence or political persecution.

Understanding this history and context can be overwhelming at first, but it ultimately leads to empathy and curiosity. When I look Tacoma in the eye, I realize that America has the propensity to exploit immigrant labor, blame immigrants whenever we don't meet profit goals, kick them out in anger, then look the other way to let in different immigrants because our economy, as currently constructed, depends on undocumented labor. I realize the pains, struggles, and losses each family experienced to get here, making it easier to understand their perspectives, values, and goals for themselves and their children. That empathy makes collaboration and peacemaking possible.

When my fellow Tacomans don't consider the planks in our eyes and the wealth generated by this repeated exploitation, they tend to look around and blame immigrants for every woe and inconvenience. They want the immigrants removed but are also not prepared to pay higher prices for goods and services that would result. Meanwhile, we are in desperate need of workers in many industries, and we also need a robust workforce paying more taxes to cover the significant costs of American entitlement programs like Social Security.

Racism

Washington State was established after slavery was abolished. The blatant Jim Crow laws of the South were not the strategy of systemic racism employed here, even though those laws contributed to the Great Migration, which led many Black Americans to move to Tacoma throughout the twentieth century. But racism was, and continues to be, a reality in Tacoma. One of the more notorious behaviors was the practice of redlining.

Figure 4.1 displays a map of Tacoma from 1937. These maps were created by banks and real estate companies and backed by the Home Owners' Loan Corporation, a federal government agency. These maps determined where people could and could not reside or attain home loans. Certain areas were deemed more desirable, and mortgages and deeds for homes in those neighborhoods were generally limited to White families. Black, Mexican, Asian, Jewish, and other groups were relegated to "hazardous" neighborhoods. These families were also excluded from access to mortgages, and these communities suffered from chronic disinvestment. Not surprisingly, the desirable regions flourished and became home to many White, wealthy families.

A 2020 study between the city of Tacoma and Ohio State University's Kirwan Institute of Race and Social Justice

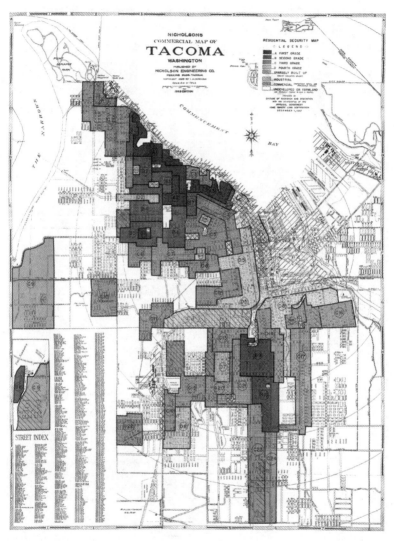

FIG. 4.1 Nicholson Engineering Co. Tacoma residential security (redlining) map, 1929 ed., updated 1937. North central properties are shown as the highest grade residential properties, with southern regions shaded as undesirable or "hazardous." *Northwest ORCA (Online Records and Collections Access), Tacoma Public Library.*

health. The newer map draws attention to a major plank in Tacoma's eye: historically redlined areas overlap with areas of reduced livability today.

Many Black families in Tacoma are familiar with this history. They know their grandparents and great-grandparents were not allowed to buy homes and were probably not allowed access to jobs that paid enough to save anything for future

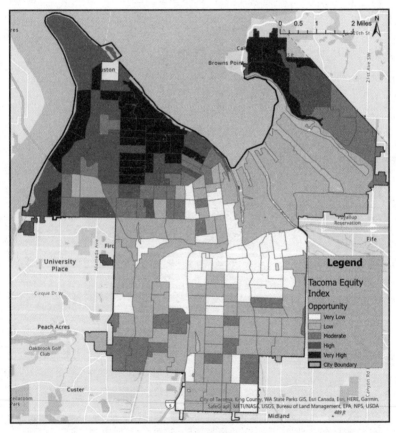

FIG. 4.2 A map representing access to opportunity in Tacoma. Darker areas represent areas of greater equity. Lower equity areas roughly align with redlined zones from nearly a century earlier. *City of Tacoma, Kevin Le, "Equity Analysis Favors Broader Home in Tacoma Rezone," January 3, 2022, https:// www.theurbanist.org/2022/01/03/spatial-equity-analysis-home-in-tacoma/.*

generations. On a level playing field, perhaps the sorting of wealthy and impoverished households would be different. But it appears that many households are prosperous today not because their ancestors worked smarter or harder but because of private and public sector policies. That is why, while those of us engaging in peacemaking might smile at a job paying just over minimum wage, households from redlined communities only tolerate pathways to living wages and other strategies or policies that will allow them to build intergenerational wealth they can pass along to their children.

REMOVING THE PLANK FROM MY EYE

As a financial coach and community economic development professional, I could advocate for a numbers-based strategy to provide economic opportunities for everyone. I can look at wages, housing prices, gentrification, the risk of future reductions in federal funding and recessions, climate change, and the continued impact of artificial intelligence and technology and identify an economic development plan. But when I take that plan to a meeting with people from the Puyallup Tribe, to a community with low homeownership rates and high poverty that was historically redlined, or to a meeting with Latin American immigrants who suspect I might be an ICE officer, what are my expectations?

I appreciate that Jesus exaggerated his metaphor. He didn't say to remove the pencil before we addressed the speck in our neighbor's eye. He said to address the plank. It's huge, it weighs us down, it's embarrassing that we haven't addressed it. The plank is so large that our concern with our neighbor's speck is laughable and will justifiably be ignored.

Fortunately, removing planks from our eyes does not require plans and solutions. It requires acknowledging and listening. What is the context and history? What do these communities want for themselves? What are their aspirations, and what do they perceive as opportunities and obstacles? There are endless strategies and competencies required to do economic peacemaking, and we should be prepared with skills and data so that we do not overpromise and underdeliver as we build trust with communities. The next chapters dig into some of these strategies.

But it is important to remember that the specifics will become clear in collaboration with the communities. The most effective strategies I have implemented have always involved communities shaping or leading the strategy. I might collect and offer information about living wage jobs, competencies, and training programs, and the community complements that information with an insider perspective about what works and what will not. Then, as daunting as all this can seem, the strategies reveal themselves. Of course, then comes the question of whether we have the ability and integrity to follow through.

DISCUSSION QUESTIONS

1. What are some of the planks in the eyes of your local community?
2. If you were to engage in economic peacemaking in your community, how might you address these planks as you are getting started?
3. If you brought someone before Jesus to be judged, what might he write in the sand that would cause you to walk away from judging others?

LOCAL ECONOMIC PEACEMAKING

A large income is the best recipe for happiness I ever heard of.
—Jane Austen, *Mansfield Park*

Welcome to the party, pal!
—John McClane, in *Die Hard*

This chapter presents opportunities and best practices for engaging in economic peacemaking in a community. Becoming an economic peacemaker is not a process of replacing the other work we do in the community with a hyper-focus on jobs and money, nor is it becoming a cadre of Christian economists and statisticians. Local economic peacemaking is about building relationships. Christians are well suited to this work. We tend to thrive at building relationships with people in the community, at least historically, and then tailoring programs or advocacy to the community's needs based on those relationships. This means our strategies are informed by cultural nuances and context that might be overlooked if you didn't have those relationships.

My church conducted a neighborhood needs assessment a few years ago because we were opening a new community center in our low-income city region as part of a larger building maintenance project. We paired up and knocked on every door in the neighborhood, building relationships and asking questions about needs. I was responsible for consolidating the feedback and presenting the data to the church leadership. To no one's surprise, housing affordability and homelessness was significant and at the top of many folks' minds. The initial discussions drifted toward how we might address housing and homelessness.

We decided to reach out to some housing and workforce development organizations, but we didn't see any programs or ministries we could run that seemed to meet the need or that we could afford. There was a feeling of angst that we had a portfolio of ministry programs based on our prior physical capacity. We'd offered those programs for decades, and they were beloved, but were they meeting the needs of the community? If a new program that addressed housing became a focal point, would it displace other programs? And how detrimental would that be to the community?

So we had more conversations, did additional research, and realized that one of our most beloved programs is a partnership with a low-income middle school just down the street. For many years, we had offered an after-school tutoring program to help lower-income middle schoolers thrive academically and provide a safe place after school before parents or caregivers could pick them up. Our research confirmed that tutoring programs are among the best investments to ensure that children grow up to be adults who can attain living wage jobs. Without those programs, children might fall into absenteeism and not even graduate high school. We realized that in the long term, this after-school tutoring program was our best contribution to the housing affordability and homelessness crisis. If we could help children become adults who obtain jobs that can enable them to afford local housing, we would have contributed to the solution. So our ongoing relationships with the community prevented us from throwing out a beloved, homegrown, genuinely anti-homelessness initiative in search of a short-term program that may or may not have any impact on homelessness.

This is the heart of economic peacemaking work. Build relationships, listen, and pay attention; the strategies reveal themselves as common sense, "aha" projects when you least expect them but are ready to see them.

SOCIAL DETERMINANTS OF HEALTH

If you have jobs but not enough housing, your strategy will be different than in a community with housing but not enough jobs. But just as with a community that lacks both housing and jobs, these communities need an economic and social ecosystem that offers the same resources and opportunities. And all these communities will have the same problem: whatever local jobs there are likely will not pay enough to afford whatever local housing there is.

One holistic framework to apply to a community that informs economic peacemaking rather than just one area of need, such as economic development, is whatever the opposite of adverse childhood experiences (ACEs) is. As described in chapter 2, the ACEs framework helps us measure how poorly we are achieving economic peacemaking goals in the long term. If parents are stressed and overworked, housing is unaffordable, and healthy food is hard to find, then other indicators such as crime and substance abuse are likely to increase, leading to more adverse experiences for more children. But we cannot just focus on removing bad outcomes from a community. What investments do we want to move toward rather than just trying to shift away from harmful things? One anti-ACEs framework that has emerged over the years is the social determinants of health, an excellent tool for identifying specific economic peacemaking strategies.

Social determinants of health are the living conditions that affect people's health, functioning, and quality of life. This can include anything from sidewalks to food to community activities and access to books. The determinants can be grouped into five domains: economic stability, neighborhood and built environment, health and well-being, education, and social equity.

This chapter digs into the first two domains; in the next, we'll look at the complementary peacemaking strategies most critical to achieve and sustain economic peacemaking outcomes. As we have noted, economics is connected to food, housing is connected to early childhood development, transportation is connected to education, which affects jobs and economics, law enforcement has a critical but limited role to play, and so on. Peacemaking that adopts an economic lens requires thinking about a range of things simultaneously, which is why this work is so relational.

ECONOMIC STABILITY STRATEGIES

I am all for generously giving to the poor, but I also like (other) sustainable solutions. And if we can reduce the number of people experiencing poverty, it better equips us to help the remaining households. The other demographic who prefer sustainable solutions are recipients of charity. Almost everyone prefers a dignified job that leads to independence and pride over depending on others to meet basic needs. That's why plan A is getting more people connected with living wage jobs—and here are some primary opportunities to do that.

Support workforce development

In the United States, workforce development systems are often federal contract management infrastructure masquerading as community-based efforts. The Workforce Innovation and Opportunity Act (WIOA) provides nationwide funding and regulation for One-Stop or WorkSource centers.[1] These centers provide résumé writing, career navigation services, and training funding. They focus on workers who lost their jobs through no fault of their own, low-income adults, and youth and young adults. Unfortunately, managing public contracts is stressful and cumbersome. So these affiliates around the country have extensive and expensive administrative staff to manage contracts and ensure reporting requirements are met.

This is a tremendous service to local communities, and we need the workforce development sector to function well so this work can be executed in the community. However, being a federal contract manager is not as alluring as some of the boisterous community engagement activities that complementary partners do, like Friday night activities for youth or food banks with families lined up at the entrance. Colleges have campuses, cities have prominent city halls, Goodwills have stores, Boys and Girls Clubs have large facilities, and United Ways hold large public fundraisers—whereas your regional workforce development stakeholder probably has a discreet office in a commercial district with a name no one recognizes.

Still, while WIOA organizations tend to be less well known, they do not have to fundraise as nonprofits do; they are flush with federal cash assigned to them. We should advocate for these systems to invest those dollars for maximum benefit in the community. Unfortunately, these workforce development agencies often try to replicate what others are doing rather than focus on providing their unique niche well.

WIOA organizations should put every dollar they can into funding training programs that lead to living wage jobs, providing high-quality career services, or getting actionable information from employers about jobs and hiring needs. Instead, many organizations host events and fund community engagement strategies with no clear goal or benefit. Years ago at a community meeting, I tried to explain why we should focus on what each of us does well rather than each organization trying to do everything, stepping on each other's toes, and competing for funding and attention from the community. We should stop being embarrassed by who we are, admit what we do well, be proud of the value of that contribution, and focus on executing that vision with excellence.

WIOA partners and centers vary by state, but they can be found in or nearby to most communities.[2] To support their efforts, we can volunteer on community advisory boards and develop relationships with local elected officials. We can ask questions about living wage jobs, employers, and competencies and expect our workforce development agencies to have answers. And when they do, we can be thankful for their critical work in the community. We can find them, get to know them, support them, and express appreciation for their efficiency and impact on training the workforce for a chaotic job market. As always, relationship-building is a core competency for economic peacemaking.

Keep the focus on living wage jobs

Helping people attain living wage jobs is extraordinarily difficult. First of all, there is no perfect definition of what a living wage is. It will vary based on region and household status. But you do not have to start a conversation with a perfect definition.

Often, lower-income families know their goals for themselves, and you can work through what it would cost to achieve and maintain those goals. But as we've discussed in earlier chapters, a good rule of thumb is not spending more than 30 percent of income on rent. Some people like to include utilities, and some want to increase it to 40 percent. To mitigate these pressures, I set the goal as 30 percent of pre-tax income. If the average rent in a community is $1,500, that means a household needs $5,000 per month in pre-tax income. That means earning $60,000 a year, or—dividing by the rule of thumb that a year of full-time work is 2,080 hours—$28.85 per hour. Now, does that wage include benefits? Is the $60,000 attainable with two income earners in the household? Perhaps families in your area have easier access to childcare, personal transportation, or public transportation, which affects these numbers. This is a fluid but productive conversation.

Regardless, you are going to end up with a number higher than what most jobs in your area pay. You will either identify $30 an hour as a living wage and realize most jobs pay $18 to $20 an hour, or you will find $15 an hour is a living wage, but most jobs pay $8 to $9 an hour. This chasm can feel daunting. A living wage is not a short-term goal for most people, but it must be the long-term desired outcome. If we stop this work when we have helped someone earn a slightly higher-paying poverty wage, we have accomplished nothing. Maybe someone is not ready for the strenuous process required to become trained for a living wage job. That's okay, a slightly higher wage might work for a while. But that is not a permanent solution. We must consider how that person will earn a living

wage in a few years. Or perhaps many people in your community are employed, but you cannot find enough living wage jobs
in the area to train people for. That's also okay—and a reason to
acknowledge this problem and start working toward a solution.

What we cannot keep doing is being satisfied and helping
people attain jobs that do not help them meet the basic needs
of their families or households. That will only compound
hopelessness and lead to less peaceful outcomes.

Engage employers and advocate for workers

I was a workforce development case manager during the Great
Recession, then a program manager and strategist for the next
decade. During the recession, an alarming dynamic grew that
we have never fully recovered from. Workers with decades of
experience who had never done anything else were abruptly
laid off. As a case manager, I would meet with six to eight clients
a day, hearing their stories and trying to figure out a plan to find
a different job or get retrained in a terrifying economic context.

Some employers had a field day. Senior-level workers were
suddenly desperate for work and willing to accept entry-level
wages. When I worked with employers five years later, many
still had that expectation. They expressed frustration with the
struggle to find workers, so I would ask how much they paid.
Some employers offered $3 to $4 over the hourly minimum
wage for jobs requiring professional certifications and training.

It turned out that helping employers understand what con-
stitutes a living wage in the area was a significant and overlooked opportunity. We would talk about profit and wages,
comparing before and after the recession. Sometimes they
would realize their profits had grown much faster than wages.
If wages had increased at the same rate, those jobs might
pay $10 or $15 more than the hourly minimum wage. When

confronted with the realization of what their profit would be if they right-sized wages, some employers scoff. They may have assumed their increased wealth was a result of their ingenuity rather than underpaying their workforce. Others, however, had no idea how much less they were paying their workers relative to the cost of living than before the recession. They took pride in caring for their workers and assumed that the wage, which looked good on paper relative to previous decades, reflected that commitment.

This is another opportunity to practice empathy. Some wealth leads to, or is a result of, a sense of entitlement, and such folks may think nothing of suppressing wages to accumulate more wealth than they actually need. For others, some wealth is just a relief after years of toil and scarcity. I am middle-aged now, and the Great Recession occurred toward the beginning of my career, so a whole generation of today's workers did not experience that economy. Some small or family business owners who are seemingly earning money hand over fist now, causing resentment among workers, struggled mightily for years. During and after the recession, housing prices plummeted, businesses failed left and right, and people walked away from mortgages because they owed way more than the homes were worth. Some employers fought and struggled for years, going without vacations or rest, and paying workers before giving themselves a paycheck. Then, things finally picked up, and they found themselves doing well. Today they might think, "Phew, finally. I survived and now I get to enjoy some of the fruits of all that sacrifice." Then they hear resentment from workers who do not know their stories, and they justifiably get defensive rather than evaluating the wages they offer.

Similarly empathetic conversations can happen around childcare. One of the largest underutilized workforces is single or stay-at-home parents, most of whom are mothers. These parents often want to work, but the economy frequently does not accommodate them. When their children are young, they want to continue to work part-time to keep investing in their skills and network and to supplement the household income. But part-time jobs are very difficult to find, especially with the inherent limitations of caregiving. Even when children are older and in school full-time, this workforce cannot reliably be at a desk from eight to five. They must drop kids off at school at nine in the morning and pick them up around three or four in the afternoon. I was a part-time stay-at-home dad for nearly eight years, and I can tell you it feels like the school is frequently closed, or at least one kid is always sick. So, yes, these parents are not as reliable if you expect someone to be at a desk for nine hours. But these workers are some of the most committed, dependable, and loyal. These moms and dads might leave at three in the afternoon to pick up kids, but if needed, they finish their work after the kids go to bed.

There is also much work to be done around measuring job effectiveness. Many jobs still track hours spent at work compared to productivity. I urge employers to stop worrying about the number of hours, focus on outcomes required for a particular job, and be happy when those goals are met. Employers, too, are having difficulty adapting to the complex world that households struggle to adapt to. Economic peacemakers must spend more time building relationships with employers to help them understand the context in which they operate and innovate. Employers should be competing to find and hire single parents, who will often work harder and produce more than many other workers. These adaptations might be wages or flexible schedules. They also might be something like providing childcare on-site or nearby.

We are often already in these relationships and don't even realize it. Employers are part of our communities. They may be in our churches or neighborhoods. Or you attend a meeting of the local Rotary club. When you do find employers, hiring managers, and small business owners, they will enthusiastically share their thoughts and concerns about hiring and retention. Just be ready to remain empathetic and curious because some of them will share from a place of frustration at first.

Support financial literacy

Financial literacy workshops and classes have become quite popular in nonprofits and high schools, but they rarely go far enough to have a sufficient impact. The credit and financial system is complex, and little can be done if someone's income is too low, so the workforce development pipeline needs to work for this even to be an option. When participants enroll in training programs for living wage jobs, we often need to help them get their credit scores up before they get a new job, especially if they will need a loan to buy a car so they can get to work.

Other needs and expectations come with a new job, so an enhanced ability to budget and plan that comes with financial coaching is critical. Many financial literacy programs raise awareness about a good credit score or how to dispute incorrect information on a credit report. It isn't easy to balance a budget and make little adjustments toward a good credit score, which can take eighteen months or two years. What communities need is akin to financial literacy case management: an ongoing relationship with a financial coach who helps track spending, monitor credit scores, and build a plan based on life goals and values. This can be expensive, although some nonprofits and financial institutions offer this service for minimum cost, or even for free in some cases. (I am a certified financial coach through the Association for Financial Counseling & Planning Education, which I chose because of its emphasis on life goals and life coaching infused with financial literacy.)

When I built a financial empowerment initiative for a local credit union, we experimented with five unique financial products offered to people who met with one of the financial coaches. We offered a $1,000 emergency loan for problems such as burst pipes in the winter, but if we exceeded a certain percentage of defaults, that product would be rescinded. We rarely encountered someone whom we thought might repay that loan who did not qualify for a personal loan elsewhere.

We had an exciting auto refinance loan to get people out of predatory 29 percent loans. Individuals could refinance for around 13 percent, freeing up some financial capacity to work on their credit score so that down the road, they could apply for a 6 percent auto loan and be home free. However, we required twelve monthly on-time payments on the existing loan in order to qualify because the tool would also be rescinded if the default rate was too high. Unfortunately, we rarely encountered applicants who qualified.

The most effective products were a checking account and an innovative one-year savings account. Many people in low-income communities turn to check-cashing institutions to access their money, partly because of a history of bounced checks and overdrafts and partly because many traditional financial institutions do not have branches in these communities. However, people who use check cashing and payday loan places spend an average of $1,000 per year on these services. We also learned that these check-cashing locations provide excellent customer service. People will pay a lot for a dignified experience over a shame-based one.

The savings account was a novel way to build credit. It was a $300 twelve-month savings account and loan. When I helped someone set one up, I would meet them at a credit union branch. We would sit down with a credit union representative, and my client would bring $300 in cash. They would hand the representative $300, and then the representative would hand a different $300 in cash to my client. Technically, it was a $300 loan collateralized by the $300 in the new savings account. The loan also had a 12 percent interest rate to help cover the costs, adding up to about $36 of interest over the year, which was primarily symbolic. My client would make twelve monthly payments of about $28. After twelve months, that $300 would be deposited into a new checking account, and those monthly payments were reported as a loan repaid. A new checking account was born, $300 was saved, and a credit score was increased. This was a popular and successful product, especially with the financial literacy case management the certified financial coaches provided.

Comprehensive case management or system change may not be feasible or interesting for many people. Still, there are some initiatives that local churches and community groups could implement. One is finding financial coaches who already provide these services and either sponsoring people from the community to meet with them or asking financial coaches to donate some time to do free consultation. Churches also have people with lots of financial knowledge and personal experience who can offer this expertise in the context of a mentoring relationship.

Some groups and individuals pool resources to help pay certain debts, especially ones in default. Defaulted loans are purchased by collection agencies for pennies on the dollar. So if someone defaulted on a $5,000 debt, an agency will purchase it for maybe $500 and try to collect the full amount. A church group might help negotiate with that collector and agree to pay $1,500 up front to discharge the debt. This is also common with medical debt.

A community activity that incentivizes savings as well as financial literacy is savings groups. Usually this involves about ten people contributing monthly to a pooled sum for ten months. Each month a different person receives the pool. You will contribute $10 a month each time, but one of those months you will receive $100. Or you contribute $100 but will receive $1,000 one time. The communal aspect can be fun and adds accountability.

However you incorporate financial literacy into an economic peacemaking strategy, it is almost always a critical part of achieving and maintaining a desired peacemaking outcome.

Understand entrepreneurship

I have managed both domestic and international entrepreneurship training programs, and the conversation is different in each context. In many communities around the world, entrepreneurship more easily makes sense. In a more remote area, you can identify a product or service unavailable in your local community. You can do the math to figure out what it would cost to transport any goods from a city to your community, how much profit you hope to earn per item or service, what the ongoing demand might be, and, therefore, what price you would sell the product for locally compared to what you purchase it for in bulk.

Western countries are more fully developed economies, and much of this low-hanging fruit has already been picked. Most products and services can be delivered to your door for low prices. Lots of people are trying to build entrepreneurial ventures as supplemental income generators. The other factor is time. It might take years to create a product, build a brand, and establish yourself with sufficient profit that this could be a full-time job. This is especially hard to do in an individualist, fully developed economy. In more collectively oriented communities or contexts, individuals might live in a compound of homes with their family and can rely on them while they work on a business.

In many Western economies, you must figure out how to pay rent and utilities and buy food each month regardless of your context and long-term plans. This often requires working multiple part-time jobs, a full-time job, and a side gig. In this context, where is the time and energy for building a business to profitability, which might require full-time effort? Much entrepreneurship training is helping people understand what it really takes to do this, allowing them to go through a grieving process and then helping them figure out a more lucrative traditional career pathway. Sometimes, a hobby turns into an income-generating activity, but that is hard to predict and depend on as a solution for a struggling household.

A nonprofit I worked with was awarded funding to get a small business/entrepreneurship loan up and running with specialized financial coaching and planning. The screening process involved working through costs, demand, and potential income from entrepreneurs' ideas. A business plan specialist met with entrepreneurs to talk about their business plans, and I processed the applications for funding and worked through the financial plans.

One day, I met with a grandmother who loved to bake cupcakes and was about to sign a three-year lease at a neighborhood commercial space that kept being vacated. It was alarming that the space was frequently occupied and vacated, but we worked through the math. Given her expenses, the lease, and the cost of making cupcakes, she would have to bake and sell around three thousand cupcakes per month at a fairly high price. She burst into tears, realizing she could not do that. She imagined a more leisurely hang-out space where people would build community and occasionally buy a cupcake or coffee. She was caring for her three young grandchildren and struggling to make it work. She imagined this cupcake store would be a safe place for her family and an income generator. We continued to work through the numbers and plan, including a longer build-up for her business that did not require that expensive lease. In later meetings, we worked on a more traditional career plan that would guarantee needed income in the near term.

When entrepreneurship is an appropriate strategy, I am a tremendous advocate for it, so we need to support entrepreneurs and make our local cities support them. Homeboy Industries in Compton, California, has been the gold standard for this work. Manchester Bidwell in Pittsburgh is a more expensive iteration but a good example to learn from. Kiva is a great way to fund domestic and international entrepreneurs who work with local organizations. Tacoma has a famous glass museum downtown and a thriving glass-blowing industry. A local nonprofit trains youth to become glassblowers and sells their work around the community. Entrepreneurship can be fun and impactful, but having realistic expectations and goals is important.

STRATEGIES FOR THE NEIGHBORHOOD: HOUSING AND INFRASTRUCTURE

I often talk about the two most important factors in economic peacemaking as two sides of a coin. One side is jobs, and the other is the cost of housing. Sometimes we can find ourselves in a tug-of-war over which is most important, but we need to work on both. Employers have more power than workers, keep wages low, and reduce workforces. We have not been building enough housing or creating conditions for sufficient housing density since the Great Recession. Working to increase wages is more of a medium-term strategy, whereas housing—which requires significant inputs of capital and time—is a long-term strategy, but all the more reason to figure out the plan sooner rather than later.

Rethink zoning

One of the most significant conversations around housing is zoning. Local and regional governments zone areas for different uses, such as commercial, agricultural, or residential. As it refers to housing, we often talk about residential zoning. There are city, region, and state regulations about how many houses can be located per acre, how tall buildings can be, how much space must be used for green space or parking. The United States has historically zoned for single-family houses, where we average one home for every five thousand square feet of land. As jobs became more concentrated in cities, this single-family zoning made it prohibitively difficult to build higher-density housing to accommodate demand. In many communities, even cities such as Tacoma and Seattle, 70 or 80 percent of all the land is for single-family houses. Not surprisingly, there is a growing movement to rethink zoning policy and redraw our maps. This may be necessary, but it has tremendous downsides to consider.

In Tacoma, the two common arguments around new zoning policies are "We don't want to become San Francisco" and "We don't want to become Seattle." California cities like San Francisco and San Jose are notorious for having fought new zoning policies that would have allowed for higher density. The result is a high quality of life and excessive housing wealth for households who owned homes before the tech boom. But there are also downsides, including more homelessness and an inability to hire for critical jobs such as teachers and grocery store workers. Those jobs do not pay enough to live in the area.

Seattle is not much different, because all the suburbs are single-family zones, but the downtown region pursued housing density. Quality of life plummeted. The housing that was created was high-end and compact. The units increased but were designed for tech industry workers without families. Homelessness increased anyway, crime went up, and now the people who do live downtown often can't do anything but stay in their homes. There are few green spaces, few public spaces not littered with tents, and few activities for those without disposable incomes. Many residents can't afford to go to downtown's theaters, coffee shops, or pubs. The implication of these arguments is that Tacoma can ignore zoning policy and become San Francisco, or we can go all in on housing density and become Seattle-light.

Like many communities, Tacoma has a lot of pride in its culture, history, and community. It's blue-collar and lower-income, under the national radar but surprisingly at the center of many historical events and movements. How do we pursue the affordable housing component of economic peacemaking without becoming a futuristic sci-fi dystopia? This will require rezoning *and* simultaneously addressing the complementary elements of the social determinants of health. Community members suspect much of the talk from public officials about infrastructure and community engagement is just paying lip service. The zoning must incorporate standards for a high quality of life, such as green spaces, sidewalks, and sufficient amenities within walking distance. And the community needs to hold elected officials accountable. In Tacoma, there is a trend of putting promises on paper about holistic infrastructure, and then city leaders often sign off on whatever exemptions developers ask for, leading to high-density, low-quality-of-life housing setups.

The housing and zoning conversation depends on context. Even in denser cities, the nuances of achieving a balanced vision for the community will vary based on culture, demographics, economics, geography, and so on. Rural communities also struggle with housing affordability, although the challenge might be related more to lower wages and limited services like high speed internet. In many communities, maintaining aging housing is as important as building new units. A growing ministry for churches is maintaining homes for seniors or adapting housing for seniors to remain in their current homes.

A city or county planning department is the home for zoning issues. These departments often send representatives to community meetings to help residents understand the plan for the community. Individuals can attend community gatherings, and groups such as Rotary clubs, neighborhood associations, and churches can invite city planners or elected officials to come discuss issues around zoning and housing. They are usually eager for opportunities, and this is a great way to influence the direction of a community.

Build accessory dwelling units

Generally speaking, addressing housing issues is a long-term effort. It takes years to acquire land, to plan a housing project, to collect sufficient approvals from the city, and to get the housing built. Highest-density housing, such as apartments and condos, is significantly slower to build and become available. Even getting a developer to commit to a project can be a challenge. When I worked for a small city of about 60,000 residents, city planners threw tax credits and exemptions at developers to get them to build . . . anything. They wouldn't need to create affordable housing or help us increase the number of units. But housing is in demand everywhere, and the construction industry has done a poor job of training and maintaining a sufficient number of workers, so developers stay in larger cities and focus on projects that pay a premium.

Workforce development is often a shorter-term effort to help households afford rent while we grind away the housing issue. Still, there are other housing solutions, including accessory dwelling units—tiny houses placed on single-family zoned lots, often alongside an existing home. ADUs increase housing density and get around a lot of the complexity of rezoning, tax incentives, and public notices. Many homeowners with larger lots would love to add an in-law or rental unit. It might generate extra income and provide housing for an aging or disabled family member, or aging owners can downsize their properties and turn the more prominent house over to their kids, who may be starting families.

Accessory dwelling units are growing in popularity but are still very challenging and expensive. Many cities do not allow them, but that is rapidly changing as affordable housing and single-family zoning conversations increase. Contractors are not yet well versed in ADUs and are unsure how to build them. This, plus the high cost of materials, makes them prohibitively expensive, at least for now. Cities are approving changes to building codes that allow an ADU, usually on several common conditions, like requiring them to be within a certain square footage and to include the same amenities as other homes.

Part of my work with the local municipality included a project to incentivize ADUs in the city. I partnered with a local financial institution and created a project outline to support broad economic peacemaking. The plan was for the city to provide seed money to the financial institution to offer homeowners 2 percent interest rate loans to build ADUs. The city would be repaid without interest as the loans were repaid, and the city would maintain a list of recommended contractors familiar with the new ADU codes the city council had just adopted. These homeowners would be approved for the loan on one condition: they would rent the new unit at no more than $100 over the monthly loan payment for the first two years, and they would rent it to a family that a local nonprofit was working with to get through a training program that we were confident would lead to a living wage job. A local organization committed to partnering with the regional technical colleges, and all the partners were eager to make this work. The financial institution would not earn much profit on this project with its 2 percent interest loans. Still, all the loans would be to reliable candidates, and they loved the idea of contributing to the community in this way.

We initially saw this as a win all the way around. This temporary housing would be a dignified way to help low-income families, especially parents, afford to get through a training program that would lead to a living wage job. The homeowners would get cheap loans and access to knowledge contracts, and while they wouldn't make much profit off rent in the first two years, the added structure would increase the value of their homes. And, at the end of two years, they could do whatever they wanted with those ADUs. If they wanted to rent them at market value to the highest bidder for whatever the market would bear, we didn't care. The city would be thrilled to increase housing density to make homeowners happy and wealthier instead of angry and anxious.

We might have been able to execute this, but there were detractors in two camps. Some homeowners loved the idea, but others were wary. I had conversations about "those people" who might live in these units and change the neighborhood's complexion. There were legitimate concerns, such as having sufficient parking if we did this at scale. The other challenge came from the utility company, which was quite skeptical that the system could handle this increase in density. Though I could never quite get the project off the ground, I still believe that ADUs or other innovative housing options can be a game changer.

Support shared housing

Some of my friends and family members have frustrating stories about tenants who refused to move out. They can intimidate owners or cause property damage. In some jurisdictions, they also have the legal upper hand. In my nonprofit work, I have encountered many elderly or disabled homeowners who were taken advantage of or abused by people who said they were just down on their luck but needed a room to rent and would pay what they could when they were able. But once those individuals moved in, they took over. To combat a rise in evictions, cities in my region have passed stricter laws about why someone can be evicted and how long it takes to do so. I empathize with the purpose of these laws, but one unintended consequence is that some cities do not distinguish between an individual with one or two units who depends on that income and a large, corporately-owned apartment complex. This counterintuitively reduces the housing stock because someone with a room to rent or an in-law unit may choose not to rent it out because of the perceived risk.

That being said, some organizations focus on shared housing as a solution for housing and economic stability. The organizations vet potential candidates; if candidates have an issue such as substance use disorder, the organizations make sure they are in treatment. The organization can provide at least some safety assurance and legal protection for the homeowner with a room to rent.

Alternatively, many people have spare rooms they are not using. Some of them may be struggling to pay their bills or may be economically stable but want to help someone in their community. This is as straightforward a solution as there is. Connect people who need housing with people who have a room to rent for a few hundred dollars a month. There are risks and downsides, but if a good organization is in place and the situation feels right, it also provides an opportunity for relationship building and sharing stories, a critical component of economic peacemaking. One Christian nonprofit in Tacoma successfully facilitates a shared housing model by setting a strict 120-day timeline and requiring that the tenants meet regularly with a social worker who ensures they progress toward attaining their own housing.

The best way to support shared housing in your community is to find an organization already doing it and learn from them. Best practices will be informed by local laws and resources. If no such organization exists in or near your community, this might indicate that gathering housing professionals, social service agencies, and community leaders to talk about this can lead to some productive conversation.

Provide lower-class and lower-middle-class housing

In 2018, the last boarding house in Tacoma closed. The very-low-income tenants were evicted, and the building was renovated into high-end condos. For some, this was an exciting development. But where did those former tenants go? A follow-up study a few years later found that almost all of them were experiencing some form of homelessness or had died.[3]

As I described in chapter 2, the boarding house was not great. They were tiny units with no kitchens or bathrooms. Each floor had a shared bathroom, and there was a shared kitchen. Many tenants had a hot plate, a mini fridge, a television, and a bed. But they were not out in the elements. The rent was $400 a month. Many tenants were seniors or had disabilities and either worked minimum-wage jobs or depended on Social Security. If you live off $800 or $1,200 per month, you would likely be thrilled to have access to a boarding house. It wouldn't be the high life, but it would be way better than living on the streets or in a car. If you struggle to earn more than that and your only option becomes a studio apartment that, while it has its bathroom and kitchen, costs $1,000 or more . . . you're in trouble.

As I discussed earlier, a critical component of economic peacemaking is a thriving lower middle class. Tacoma's complex building codes ruled out new boarding houses or other, less expensive alternatives for lower-class housing. The unintended consequence is more and more tents on our sidewalks and RVs parked in commercial districts. Is that better? Is it preferable for someone who maybe just went through a divorce and is working a minimum wage job while they go through a hard time to be forced to live in a tent or to have a dignified housing option they can afford so they have a platform to bounce back from when they can? I have had hard times financially, and I would have joyfully taken a tiny room with a gross shared bathroom for a time while I figured things out, rather than struggle to pay for an apartment with amenities that were less important to me at that time than trying to find stable financial footing.

We have also limited options for entry-level and lower-middle-class housing. Developers are building high-end micro apartments, condos, and larger houses because those provide maximum profit. The profit margins for moderate-sized, entry-level, and lower-class housing will be lower, like a modern version of boarding houses. Therefore, it can challenging to recruit developers to build housing options for broader range of income brackets.

Furthermore, acknowledging the need and building for a thriving lower class and lower middle class is likely to receive initial pushback from the community. Over time, this can be overcome by explaining this is the best alternative to homelessness. Someone living in moderately sized and priced housing is still participating in this system with the rest of us, and there is some stability and hope that we can work with and keep figuring things out. If that person is in a tent, they are pulling at the threads of community systems. Our only alternatives right now are a lot more prisons and populist authoritarian leaders, which is the opposite of peacemaking.

Churches have a long history of trying to meet housing needs. Some congregations own local housing units or manage their own homeless shelters. For a time, many churches started using their land for RVs to park, but they have pulled back on that since they also tend to run youth group activities in the same space. In my community, a Catholic organization bought an apartment complex and negotiated a reduction on property taxes in exchange for lower rents and support for households. They hired a community manager who lives on-site and helps those families get connected to resources and training so that they can find permanent housing elsewhere.

A faith-based nonprofit in Tacoma provides services for low-income households and tries to help the various faith communities work together. A few years ago the city created an affordable housing action strategy that emphasized providing housing for households earning 80 percent of the median household income. This nonprofit advocated for an emphasis on households earning 30 percent of the median income, which represents a large percentage of struggling households. There are many opportunities to provide housing for lower-income households if we start looking for them.

Engage infrastructure

The issue of infrastructure, the physical and organizational structures that allow a community to function, is surprisingly polarizing and closely connected to economic peacemaking outcomes, both directly and indirectly. Infrastructure is an obstacle and opportunity that needs to be addressed to build higher-density housing. It will also be an obstacle to peacemaking if infrastructure is ignored and housing density is pursued anyway. If you have been involved in infrastructure conversations in your community, you know how complex and frustrating this issue is to people. Anyone who has lived in a community not built on car dependency knows what a more robust infrastructure looks like. Communities with high walkability and excellent public transportation are generally superior to communities where you must get in a car whenever you want to buy groceries or go to a park.

Still, most cities in the United States were constructed to be car-dependent. The houses are in the suburbs, jobs are in the cities, and businesses and amenities in central locations. We do a lot of driving and sitting at traffic lights or in traffic on the freeways looking for parking, paying for parking, and parking on roads. Cars take up an enormous percentage of land that could be used for green spaces, public amenities, and housing. So naturally, the conversation is, let's become more like the cities that are not so car-dependent. Therefore, the plan is to increase housing density and remove parking spots. This might make sense, except we do this in communities built for car dependency without an alternative infrastructure plan.

As a member of a local community advisory board, I'm deeply involved in discussions on infrastructure. With jobs increasingly centralizing in urban areas, both urban and suburban infrastructure are stretched thin, leading to significant traffic congestion. Many areas with adequate infrastructure suffer a lack of job opportunities, driving residents to move to cities and suburbs in search of work. This influx results in overcrowded schools, libraries, parks, and community centers. Public transportation in most cities often falls short, with buses taking an hour for a trip that could be a ten-minute drive. Without addressing the infrastructure choices of the past, increasing housing density through rezoning will only worsen the quality of life in cities. When this happens, households with means will leave those communities, resulting in a high density of lower-income households and insufficient tax revenue. When communities most need good schools, buses, parks, and libraries, cities close them down because of low tax revenue.

Concerns over infrastructure are sometimes used in bad faith to undermine housing construction or rezoning policies. Residents are less likely to say "I just don't want my community to change at all," "I want housing scarcity so the value of my home keeps going up," or "I don't want people who look different than me moving here." Instead they express worries about traffic or classroom sizes. Economic peacemakers do not want to make the mistake of dismissing these complementary issues.

On the one hand, housing affordability is a crisis and we must build, incentivize, or allow as much housing as possible. On the other hand, as a parent, I am also compelled to consider what the community will look like in ten and twenty years. Unfortunately, because we have such a lengthy community engagement and approval process in the United States, we spend much more money on projects than communities in other Western countries. For instance, high-speed rail projects are prohibitively expensive and slow to build. The United States does not have a strong bus culture or sufficient bus infrastructure. To unlock a community's willingness and enthusiasm to invest in housing density, we must invest in complementary infrastructure to maintain or enhance the quality of life. As we progress, we must decide how many grocery stores we need per square mile. How many parks do we need per resident? How many community centers, libraries, coffee shops, and yes, ice cream stores? To simultaneously become less car-dependent and more locally sustainable. This can be a hard conversation with angry or fearful people on all sides, but it is where great economic peacemaking opportunity awaits.

Economic development strategies and policies are important considerations to build a thriving community, but this is also a good place to remember that we aspire to make peace, not just wealth. Peacemaking is a comprehensive labor of love. Good jobs, good systems to train for them, and reliable infrastructure to get to and from work are important, but those factors alone do not make peace. There are different definitions of what a thriving community looks like, and many factors that contribute to those visions. As we'll explore in the next chapter, some of those factors are especially important to consider if we want to evolve economic development into economic peacemaking.

DISCUSSION QUESTIONS

1. What is the conversation in your community around housing, zoning, and infrastructure?
2. Who are the workforce or economic development stakeholders in your community?
3. What are the training providers in your region, and what do you know about the programs they offer?
4. What employers are you aware of that currently pay a living wage? Which ones currently do not but should?

COMPLEMENTARY PEACEMAKING STRATEGIES

Once thoroughly broken down, who is he that can repair the damage?

—Frederick Douglass, *My Bondage and My Freedom*

One cannot think well, love well, sleep well, if one has not dined well.

—Virginia Woolf, *A Room of One's Own*

Community economic development does not displace the other work we do in the community. It enhances those efforts and reinforces other outcomes. However, economic peacemaking requires making progress in these key areas simultaneously. Our communities have become increasingly complex ecosystems, and it simply does not work to achieve outcomes in one area and deal with the rest later. This is daunting but also exciting. Communities are eager for ambitious outcomes and a little pragmatism backed up with a little audacity. People respond well to being challenged to a high standard if provided with the autonomy, support, and resources they need to achieve or surpass that standard.

Different sources are inconsistent with precise terminology and categories regarding the social determinants of health, as defined in chapter 5. Sometimes there are six or seven categories. The World Health Organization has a list of ten. This speaks to the complexity of our communities and the difficulty of balancing project goals without leaving out complementary dynamics necessary to achieving meaningful and sustainable outcomes. However, in recent years the categories have consolidated into five generally agreed-upon categories: economic stability, neighborhood and built environment, health and well-being, education, and social equity.

The previous chapter covered the first two as they directly pertain to economic peacemaking. This chapter focuses on the other three, with the goal to develop an instinct to think beyond just the math of jobs and the cost of living. Many factors must be considered in each of these categories for a community to be healthy and thriving, but we'll focus on the factors most critical for long-term economic peacemaking.

HEALTH AND WELL-BEING
Focus on children and youth
A few years ago, I worked on a project related to early childhood education. A local hospital system approached our group to help them implement a "5210 initiative." These community initiatives seek to help lower-income families achieve four primary goals for children: each day, eat at least five servings of fruits and vegetables; have no more than two hours of screen time per day; get at least one hour of play per day; and consume zero sugary drinks and drink more water.

Variations of this initiative include complementary goals such as eight hours of sleep, but those four primary outcomes are always the same. Healthcare providers are quite concerned about the trajectory of American children, and rightly so. Physical and mental health metrics do not inspire confidence. Many children watch a lot of TV and spend a lot of unrestricted time on phones, consume a lot of processed foods, drink a lot of sugary "kids" drinks, and do not get sufficient exercise or social time. This suggests a future generation of unhealthy adults who are extremely expensive to provide care for in a system that already struggles to recruit and retain professionals. Without overlooking the broader need for healthcare reform, 5210 initiatives can be an effective tool for supporting health in many communities. So when our local hospital system offered to partner with us, we jumped at the chance to do something good.

The hospitals proposed an expensive awareness campaign with radio commercials, online ads, and physical flyers distributed in low-income neighborhoods. Given our work with leaders in the community, we predicted this might not be well received—in fact, we feared it might have the opposite effect. The obstacle we were trying to overcome was probably not a lack of awareness of the benefits of these goals but an inability to attain them. This proposed campaign might be perceived as clueless and patronizing, increasing bitterness rather than understanding.

To their credit, the hospital system heard that feedback and allowed us to try something different. We used their funding for mini-grants for people in target communities. They could apply for around $1,000 to address at least one 5210 goal. We promoted this grant in communities and with childcare providers. The application was simple but required a narrative about the community's obstacles to achieving one of these goals, how these funds would help overcome these obstacles, and a basic budget to explain how these funds would be used.

This process might empower community members to solve some problems, but it would undoubtedly raise our awareness as peacemakers about opportunities and challenges that might not have been on our radar.

The proposals were fascinating. There was a lot of desire for community gardens. Gardens get children outside and mitigate screen time, and children can prepare and eat what they grow. However, communities struggled to purchase tools and resources to keep gardens going and get kids involved. Many groups requested essential gardening tools, seeds, lumber, and soil. In one instance, the issue was the area between an apartment complex and a community garden was often flooded, so the grant request was for rain boots so children could access the existing garden. Some people identified paved areas where children could play and requested tools or toys to make them accessible. A basketball hoop and some balls are not a tremendous investment, but insider knowledge about where to install the hoop and identifying someone who can manage it and hold on to the basketballs is priceless.

In economic peacemaking, there are shorter-term strategies, such as access to food, medium-term ones, such as workforce development, and long-term efforts, such as housing and zoning. But our best long-term investment, far and away, is supporting children and youth. Parents need sufficient opportunities to provide stable housing, access to healthy food, opportunities for safe relationships with other children, and time and places for play.

We can get to know and support organizations that help parents understand child development's social and emotional milestones, that help ensure community safety so kids can play, and that advocate for more grocery stores, parks, and libraries. Some excellent organizations provide preventative healthcare, dental care, academic support, and mentorship. Teachers, volunteers, youth workers, and childcare providers are essential to the long-term economic peacemaking strategy. This also means supporting our public school systems and advocating for a better funding system than our current locally-funded system, which ensures schools in low-income communities struggle the most to achieve excellent outcomes.

Support food access

Once while I was managing human services funding, a council member floated the idea of reallocating all the budget for a host of community programs directly into building affordable housing. Affordable housing and homelessness were so critical that we could not afford to spend money on anything else, at least for a while. I empathized with the idea, but I suspected there would be unintended consequences that we could not anticipate. After that meeting, I talked with providers of local food banks. They all pointed out the same potential downside. New demographics had started using the food banks. In particular, seniors and moderate-income households with children were coming to the food banks for the first time.

The food bank providers pointed out that wages in the region were stagnant, but rent was increasing dramatically. If your rent increases dramatically and you are already struggling to pay it, something has to give. Find more affordable rent is tough, and moving is expensive. There's the time spent on moving, packing, and unpacking. You might pay movers and upfront move-in costs. For many families, moving isn't really an option. But if you're already on a tight budget, what else can give?

It turns out that food banks provide a release valve for households that haven't used one before. A household can dramatically reduce spending on food but still obtain the food they need. The food bank providers in my community saw themselves as a direct homelessness mitigation partner. If they were defunded and then had to decrease services, we would accelerate the timeline in which currently housed people can become unhoused.

This is not a perfect one-to-one example, but it illustrates the broader economic ecosystem. Access to healthy food is critical, especially so that children have the nutrition, energy, and focus to succeed in school and then contribute to the stability of the community as adults. But access to food also has an immediate economic peacemaking impact that we would not want to overlook.

Address addiction and substance use disorders

A few years ago, there was an unfortunate conversation in the Seattle-Tacoma region about substance use disorders and homelessness. Local media outlets claimed that all people experiencing homelessness were using substances. Therefore, they said, homelessness is a result of choosing drugs over jobs and responsibility. There are instances where this is the case. But others are individuals who were injured on the job and prescribed opioids that lead to heroin addictions. Some are parents who lost their children and fell into depression. The LGBTQIA+ community is overrepresented among youth experiencing homelessness because they are sometimes rejected by their families and forced to leave home. Some are veterans struggling with post-traumatic stress disorder. Some have mental health disorders that make holding down a job very difficult, especially a good-paying job.

This is another opportunity to break out of simple narratives, because while the issue of substance use disorders is complex, it is a significant problem and prevents economic peacemaking outcomes. And we have a complicated history with substances and how we address them. In the United States, we have the failed history of prohibition in our past, the costly failed war on drugs, and the ineffective Drug Abuse Resistance Education (DARE) campaign.

Addiction and substance use disorders are among the most difficult complementary issues to address in a local context. Prevention is critical because the comprehensive support and care people often need to overcome an addiction is very expensive, often more than local resources can sustain. The other categories of the social determinants of health are important preventative measures. Though this remains an intractable problem in many communities and families, we do have a wealth of research and resources about ways to provide effective, trauma-informed care for people and communities suffering from addiction and other substance-related disorders.

Attend to mental health

Like substance use disorders, the issue of mental health is enormous and has many facets, but I will highlight one piece of advice I give to all of my students: to get off social media. (In the classroom, I refer to it as *anti*social media.)

It is increasingly clear that social media is detrimental to our mental health. It makes it difficult to determine what is true and what is untrue, where sources of information originate, how biased they are, and whether they consider context and culture. Social media matches us with like-minded people rather than giving us access to diverse opinions, and then, in our newly formed tribes, it feeds us outrage and anxiety. It also effectively forces us to compare ourselves with the best versions of other people. Social media can make it look like everybody else is living their best life. Traveling, buying homes, having kids, always happy, always partying, constantly growing. Everyone is confident; everyone knows what is true. Everyone has unique insights and wisdom. And me. I'm scrolling on a Thursday night because I'm tired from my job, which feels like it wastes time and doesn't provide enough money for me to do anything else but scroll.

Avoiding things that harm mental health is important when so many people and companies are fighting for our attention. We also need to advocate for and practice good habits that support mental health. I suspect part of why we stigmatize mental health is because many behaviors that support good mental health are not consumption-based. Consuming content might be fun, or a break from something else that is stressful, but it is not restful. Excessive shopping might be a fun dopamine hit, but it does not help mental health, especially when we get the credit card statements. Binge-watching shows is a lot of fun, and maybe a good way to decompress, but it will not help build mental health. We need a Sabbath, a rest. We need to be in communities and physically with other people. We need to experience boredom and embrace unproductive time that leads to silence or grabbing a book we haven't read in a long time. That is all very hard to do, especially if you are a parent, work multiple jobs to pay the rent, or are worried about whether you will be able to afford a vehicle repair.

Mental health is compounding, because if we truly rest, we are better equipped to invest in our skills and capacity to care for ourselves and serve others. Economic peacemakers are often eager to list all the living wage jobs and training programs in an area and walk around with a sign-up sheet.

We might hear single parents talk about how they are fall-ing behind each month, and we get excited because we feel like we have the solution. Then we get frustrated when few people from the community immediately enroll in programs. Fatigue and a sense of hopelessness lead to short-term think-ing. Households just trying to get through each day and each month struggle to take proactive action that will pay off in one or two years.

People in the community will have ideas about how to invest in mental health, so we should listen and look for opportunities to empower them to implement those ideas.

EDUCATION

My time in international community development taught me to love education as a complementary strategy. Across the globe, one of the best and most helpfully disruptive investments is to educate young girls in particular. Education leads to asking good questions, finding sustainable solutions, and challeng-ing systems that are outdated or exploitative. It encourages thriving members of the community who approach issues with empathy and pragmatism. And it's not just limited to pre-K through college classrooms—it's important to consider wholistic and often overlooked education strategies.

Support local journalism

A critical strategy to achieve and maintain economic peace-making is committing to pay for or otherwise support local journalism. It is an alternative to the outrage and biased social media and cable news information. We need well-researched, well-written, unbiased, locally informed journalism to help us understand what is happening comprehensively and in nuanced ways. We cannot think everything is perfect or terrible because we do or do not like a particular political leader. We cannot let ourselves believe that the path to peacemaking is to defeat the other tribes.

The free(ish) information online has decimated local journalism. Much that remains has been purchased by national conglomerates that require emphasizing political messages. The unintended consequence of unbiased, comprehensive journalism is that it would make us uncomfortable in ways we have become unaccustomed to. Imagine reading a story about a local issue and realizing you were wrong about an aspect of it. Taking in information that we might disagree with initially is a muscle to be conditioned. We might be surprised how much social media has conditioned us to hear information and see images and videos affirming what we're afraid of and that we were right to be frightened.

This is a little thorny, because supporting local journalism often means supporting media that promote Christian values. That's a slippery slope to idolatry: it puts Christians in a position to decide what is true based on what we want to be true in the moment. Solid journalism will sometimes make us uncomfortable because there are always some things about the world that are true that we may not like or struggle to understand. One interesting example I keep an eye on from my state is FāVS News (formerly Spokane Faith and Values News), started by a journalism professor unimpressed by local coverage of regional and national events. She had also been exposed to perspectives from people of other faiths and loved the experience of growing from hearing those difference perspectives. This particular news outlet seems to mostly cover religious and church-centric news rather than providing comprehensive local news, but they do seem to adhere to journalistic integrity.

Support digital literacy

Even a decade ago, when I was developing apprenticeship programs for specific jobs and industries, manual labor jobs were becoming technological jobs or required a technological component. One employer lamented that finding maintenance workers for large office buildings was tough because the role of the maintenance worker was changing from more manual labor to also maintaining the energy efficiency of the building. Many jobs that might pay a living wage require digital or technical skills and the ability to learn new ones quickly.

Digital tools such as email and Microsoft Office are crucial, but so are digital collaboration tools, database management, communication tools, or at least the ability to collaborate with people who are experts with those tools. Paying bills, monitoring your credit score, applying for jobs, and paying taxes increasingly require digital literacy. Social media is oriented toward consumption; it does not require learning how to build, utilize, and manipulate these tools. Many households have smartphones but no home computers or the ability to learn digital literacy. High-speed internet is not available in many areas, and a lack of competition means it is often unaffordable when it is.

Fortunately, this is one area that is growing, and many churches are already involved. Since I am an elder at a Presbyterian Church (U.S.A.) congregation, I am more familiar with some of the tools we use.[1] Some of this training is about community building online, and others offer digital literacy training to the community. Black Churches 4 Digital Equity is an example of a faith-based initiative to address the digital divide, with initiatives to increase access to the internet and to equip Black churches to achieve digital inclusion in communities.

AI-proof the workforce

Artificial intelligence is a wild card that will disrupt our best economic peacemaking strategies. It will transform the global economy in ways we do not fully understand. That is another reason why I urge economic peacemakers to increase our empathy and curiosity: so we can pay attention and adapt our strategies and stories as changes occur.

AI will come for white-collar jobs in addition to blue-collar ones. Some jobs will be created in emerging industries that leverage technology, but will they create more jobs than they displace? And if the skills required for emerging or preserved jobs are unrelated to the experience workers attained from displaced jobs, what is our plan to mitigate this damage? Will we need to draw on plan B strategies like universal basic income?[2] Will we descend into authoritarianism as formerly middle-class workers support whatever candidate is willing to exploit their situation? We must proactively understand what economic opportunity will look like and prepare our communities for that world.

There are a couple of directions this AI-proofing could go. One is to remain competitive in industries that AI will disrupt. Routine or repetitive tasks will be easier to replace with emerging technology, but skills such as emotional intelligence, creativity, collaboration, interpersonal communication, adaptability, and cultural intelligence will become even more valuable.[3] The other direction is to equip community members with hard skills that will not be replaceable with AI. We still need people, and lots of them, to become the next generation of plumbers, electricians, and HVAC workers. There are individual churches that partner with local agencies to offer training programs and support services, but two of the most prominent examples of faith-based organizations that provide this kind of training at scale are Catholic Charities and Lutheran Community Services.

SOCIAL EQUITY

The hard part about this social determinant of health is recognizing where the economic peacemaker can contribute directly, and where the work is to remove obstacles so that community members can do this work. About a decade ago I partnered with a large agency to do community engagement in my city to understand why life expectancy was so much lower than in other parts of the city. After about six months of community conversations and surveys, we consolidated the data into five recurring themes. Three were about jobs and infrastructure, and two were about community activities and access. A debate occurred about whether the community had said organizations were responsible for all five, or whether they'd said the city and organizations were responsible for the first three so that the community could organize. The "do all five ourselves" group won out, in part because the infrastructure challenges were hard, and community dinners were planned by outside organizations. Very few people attended, and the project shut down.

Seek out a community's voice

The 5210 project described at the beginning of this chapter turned out to be an opportunity to demonstrate the value of working with the community, rather than just in or for the community. Community members told us they would love to provide more fruits and vegetables, but low-income communities are disproportionately in "food deserts"—areas with few if any places to access affordable, healthy food. If you don't have personal transportation or a grocery store nearby, much of your food is purchased from corner markets. When you are low-income you tend to prioritize the maximum number of calories per dollar over nutritional value. Corner stores rarely offer vegetables, but they might have bananas or apples for $1.25 each (a considerable markup). Or you could buy two warm hot dogs off the heat lamp rollers for 99 cents. Will your child feel fuller after one banana or two hot dogs, plus a lollipop with the remaining 25 cents to make her happy?

Similarly, parents and caregivers in the 5210 focus community knew that too much screen time was not healthy, but they already worked multiple part-time jobs to make ends meet, and they were tired from years of struggling. Time is expensive in our current system, and these parents earn close to the minimum wage per hour worked. Screens are, regrettably, a cheap babysitter. There are activities at community centers or churches in some areas, but who will take the kids to and from these activities, especially if parents are working or do not have a car? Parents would love for their children to get more exercise, even for "selfish" reasons. As a parent, I love it when my kids run around because they are entertaining themselves (which gives me a break), and they come back tired out (which gives me a break and makes it easier to get them to sleep later). But if you live in an apartment complex with gangs, drugs, and violence, you don't let your kids play outside unsupervised. That adds to the pressure to use screen time.

Reducing sugary drink consumption is another 5210 target. Families know that tap water is cheaper than buying two-liter bottles of soda or sugary juice. An awareness campaign about the savings of drinking tap water would be unnecessary. But there could be use for a campaign that raises awareness about the safety of local tap water. Low-income communities are often understandably suspicious of tap water, having heard about lead and other toxins in the pipes, or residents might come from countries where you cannot drink water from the faucet. Ensuring and celebrating the tap water quality, if you can authentically do so, could have helped the sponsoring hospital achieve this 5210 goal. But knowing this requires building relationships with the community to get this nuanced, contextual insight. One grant application asked for reusable bottles so kids could fill up and have easy access to water.

This insight is critical. Local economic peacemaking solutions will be similar everywhere but vary based on each context. In cities and more urban suburbs, you might find yourself closer to good jobs, training providers, and amenities such as hospitals and shops. However, the land is probably scarce; infrastructure is already strained, and housing is unaffordable because of all the people moving to the city looking for jobs, and the cost of living is generally higher. You might be in a more rural community with more land and where housing is relatively affordable. But even then, many rural communities are experiencing rapid rises in living costs relative to local wages because people are selling their homes in costly urban areas and moving inland.

Ultimately, what economic peacemaking strategies we emphasize may not be as critical as how we partner with the community to implement them. Each family and community will have a different vision for what it means to be peacefully thriving.

Practice storytelling and empathetic listening

If you have ever had the experience of getting mad at someone else's driving behavior, only to realize you know the person, you've experienced the power of story and empathy, especially if that person turns out to be a friend or family member. One moment you identify the stranger with the car they're driving more than their humanity and you think the worst of them, and the next moment you are flooded with empathy because their driving behavior is only one small part of their identity. Perhaps you have had an experience of being that driver because you were late for an important meeting, you were distracted worrying about something, or you were driving on a new road and got confused. Maybe other drivers were honking and gesturing, and you might think, hey, most of the time, I'm a considerate person and a great driver. They'd calmly move on if they knew the story of what was going on that day.

If you have someone in your family with mental health issues or addiction, you might find yourself defending them to other people because they don't understand the full context. If only people knew what was actually going on, they'd be empathetic and we'd all be better off.

With a few exceptions, it is a mostly universal experience that when you learn someone's story you no longer feel bitterness toward their behavior. It starts to make sense. You might hear about abuse, or loss, or different cultural values. You put yourself in their shoes and realize you might behave the same way under the same circumstances. As you are in relationship with someone longer, you might get frustrated at their behavior again, but for different reasons. You care about them, you want what's best for them, and you know what they're capable of. It's frustrating when someone you care about is not living up to their potential. But that frustration comes across differently to the other person than a stranger's. They can usually tell the difference between someone frustrated because they know their story and someone who is frustrated because of bias or projection.

Our church hosts an annual men's retreat. One year, we chose not to invite guest speakers or external people. We invited people from the church community to share their stories. It was raw and awkward because many men are generally not practiced at telling stories, let alone their own. But it was powerful. This has become standard practice at each retreat and has evolved somewhat. We started asking them to discuss topics through the lens of their stories, and we have gotten better at framing those questions.

Every year, everyone at the retreat admits there is no other time or place during the rest of the year when their guard is down and they are ready to be vulnerable enough to tell and hear stories. Even with our children, we might be vulnerable, but we don't tell stories. We especially do not tell stories with a clear goal or theme. But even when storytelling is unpracticed, it is a powerful tool. One that we tend to keep at the bottom of our toolboxes. But suppose we start practicing the art of storytelling and do more storytelling with each other and with the community. In that case, we will build relationships and see opportunities that make the path to economic peacemaking clear. And the most fun part about that dynamic is the best paths are the ones we least expect. Seeing an opportunity to make an unexpected impact is a lot of fun.

The best practice for storytelling for economic peacemaking is to listen to the stories of the various stakeholders and, while honoring the privacy and agency of the storytellers, sharing those stories with others. This is not just telling stories from low-income communities, but sharing in those communities about what is going on the broader community. There is a story about what elected officials are doing and not doing, and why. There are stories about what people in wealthier communities are doing or not doing, and why. The more we can spread stories, the more we can invoke empathy and collaboration.

We're often not accustomed to telling stories. But storytelling is far and away the best strategy to increase our capacity for empathy and curiosity. Listening to and telling stories helps us get beyond the outrage and the simple narratives to work together on complex issues and achieve economic peacemaking goals that might look different than we thought they would when we started down the path.

Public safety

Law enforcement is a critical component of peacemaking. Well-run police departments are eager to partner with other organizations to minimize their workload when needed. When I worked for a local city, we partnered with our police department to implement some strategies supported by the "defund the police" movement, while denouncing that movement's terminology, because that is some of the worst marketing language I have heard in a long time. "Defund the police" sounds like it is anti–law enforcement when, in reality, it is about law enforcement specialization. Hold law enforcement accountable to a high standard. But beyond that, let law enforcement do what it does well, and don't ask it to do what it does poorly. If there is a threat of violence in the community or violence has already occurred, law enforcement has a vital role to play. But law enforcement is generally not preventative.

I do not have a criminal background, so the fear of being arrested is a factor in my behavior, but I'm also not at high risk of choosing behaviors or being in contexts that would put me in contact with the police. People who steal, sell drugs, break into cars, and so on often have an economic or social reason for doing so. They probably have already interacted with the police and may have a criminal record. Therefore the prospect of getting arrested may not be a deterrent for future behavior. As I described in chapter 1, the dads I work with are trying to live a life that keeps them separate from law enforcement engagement. But that only works as long as they have hope that different behaviors will lead to a better outcome. That is not something law enforcement can establish if jobs are insufficient, the cost of housing is too high, or people cannot afford food or transportation. If too many people accumulate adverse childhood experiences, crime will increase.

Law enforcement may help clean up some of those messes, but peacemakers are much more concerned with preventing some of these messes. I know a percentage of the community will always engage in these behaviors, but part of the goal of economic peacemaking is achieving a high ratio of flourishing. Is, say, 80 percent of the community doing well enough to collectively engage with the remaining 20 percent who behave in destructive ways?

One of our primary investments when I worked for a local city was using some human services funding to hire a mental health professional, who partnered with an unarmed officer to respond to 911 calls in the community about mental health issues without a threat of violence. If somebody was experiencing a mental health issue, clearly had a substance use disorder, or was simply experiencing homelessness, having an armed police officer with no mental health training might result in an arrest and criminal record for someone already experiencing homelessness, which only makes that problem more challenging to overcome. The mental health professional would respond with the officer and could connect individuals to resources in the community to meet the actual need. The pilot initiative was so successful that the police department requested matching funds to hire two additional mental health professionals to meet the need. Many other communities have implemented similar or other trauma-informed responses for public safety.

This is an opportunity to practice avoiding simple narratives about whether the police are the solution or the problem. We must hold police officers accountable to a high standard and should educate ourselves about the prison industrial complex. Public safety departments who meet high standards of transparency and accountability should be partners in peacemaking, and we should respect their critical role as peacekeepers when we have failed to create an environment where they are less needed.

The range of complementary strategies in this chapter—from programs that offer water bottles to supporting digital literacy—illustrates why economic peacemaking is thrilling but not for the faint of heart. It can be overwhelming to realize that if we are going to be peacemakers and enhance our peacemaking efforts with community economic development strategies, it requires doing a lot of things well that we were previously doing okay. It would fail if we were to do this work with judgment or bitterness. If we do it with faith, hope, and love, we will achieve results faster, better, and more sustainably than expected.

DISCUSSION QUESTIONS

1. What is something in your community that complements economic peacemaking that you may not have realized was connected to economics?

2. What might it look like to increase empathy and curiosity in your community? How does that change

how you view the community? How might you take the initial steps to do this?

3. How might AI or other novel technology directly affect your community or the industries there?

POLICIES FOR PEACEMAKING

Any change may bear seeds of benefit. Seek them out. Any change may bear seeds of harm. Beware.
—Octavia Butler, *Parable of the Sower*

You do not realize that Taco Bell was the only restaurant to survive the franchise wars. So, now all restaurants are Taco Bell.
—Lenina Huxley, in *Demolition Man*

For years, I regularly held financial literacy workshops at high schools and community colleges, Rotary clubs, and youth-serving organizations. Every time I did a presentation, a moment would come when I could feel the tension rise in the classroom. We would be talking about the complexity of the credit system—the market that the three big companies Equifax, Experian, and TransUnion have over this system, the lack of regulation and clarity about the system, the ease with which information can be stolen, and the complexity of getting a good score. Growth of the importance of the credit score and its effect on your ability to attain housing and, in some instances, a job.[1]

It never happened at the same exact moment, but I could always feel it when it did. Everyone tensed up with a collective realization: *This is not a sound system; I don't understand. This is a lousy system that I have to survive until we fix it.* In those sessions, I finally learned to stop and say, Yes, you probably think this is a ridiculous system we have, and we should replace it with something more common sense that works for us better. And they would nod their heads, acknowledging, Oh, yes, that is what we're thinking. And I would say, I agree with you. But in the meantime, it's important to understand our system so you don't fall through the cracks. So that more of us can work together on replacing it with a better system, whatever that might be.

The same process happens in every facet of economic peacemaking. The stock market reflects the wealthy and not the economy overall. The housing market is more about profit for people invested in real estate and developers than ensuring people have access to shelter. Too few jobs pay a living wage. And the systems we had in place to ensure competitive wages have been removed. The healthcare system is expensive and notoriously broken. We have car-dependent communities increasing housing density and not investing in infrastructure. Communities of color were redlined and countless Black and Brown households excluded from the housing market. Then, after the prices went up, these households were permitted into the market, but encountered claims of colorblindness in a system based on racism. The United States depends on immigration for the economy to function, but many Americans want to restrict immigration. Finally, we are concerned about the federal debt but don't want to tax the wealthy.

At some point, you realize your goal is to make a cake, but you do not have the essential ingredients. You must go and acquire the ingredients that you need. Or you can bake something else with the ingredients that you have. The latter strategy is what we have adopted for many years. We shift more wealth to the wealthy and clear out the unions, the infrastructure crumbles, wages are suppressed, and the housing and stock markets are elevated. Eventually, fewer and fewer ingredients are left. Eventually, if you're trying to make an economic peacemaking cake, you have to stop and realize that at least part of your time, if not your whole career, needs to be dedicated to ensuring we have the flour and the sugar and the oven and the heat.

Local economic peacemaking is relatively easier because we have more shared values than we realize. But there is only so much you can get done. Many local economic peacemaking strategies are buying us time to address national issues. Many communities do not have enough living wage jobs for everybody who needs one. Many communities have lost their factories and employers to automation or international competition.

At the national and even state level, the differences in values and the tribal effect of simple narratives and outrage are much more significant. Millions of professing Christians in the United States believe one cannot be a Christian without equal allegiance to a particular political icon or value. And that influences allegiances and values down the list.

In this context, the recommendations and explorations in this chapter might feel like a breath of fresh air. Some people will feel their walls coming down and curiosity rising, but others might clench their fists because the ideas seem to contradict a value or a nuanced perspective or data point. I ask you to consider this chapter with both skepticism and curiosity, regardless of whether this feels like it confirms or contradicts your perspective. I suspect that everyone who reads this chapter will feel the urge at some point to say, What about. . . ? I have that reaction myself to these ideas, and am always going back and forth, questioning myself and trying to seek other views from informed advocates.

We cannot continue to wait for perfect solutions or unassailable arguments. Obstacles and opportunities to economic peacemaking must be addressed at a national and state level if we are to have the tools or autonomy to go further in our local communities.

ECONOMIC POLICIES

Whatever work we might be doing in the local community, whether connecting people with good jobs, advocating for zoning changes, supporting seniors or children, or other tasks, there comes a time when you will have that same realization my students have about financial literacy. In many ways, we are not helping people thrive in this economy but assisting families to survive this unequal economic system. At the same time, we are working to figure out how to advocate for one that provides more equitable opportunity. There are a range of economic policies to consider. I'd like to talk about some of the more puzzling challenges to implementing solutions.

Redefine a "good" economy

As I explored in earlier chapters, there is no perfect set of instruments for measuring the health of an economy. Ideally, we would be able to measure both the health of the economy for lower-middle-class and middle-class households, as well as measure indicators of economic opportunity. There are some historical measures of socioeconomic mobility and how often people transition into or out of the middle or higher classes, but those are more retrospective than a snapshot of what is currently happening. Other countries have used imperfect metrics such as happiness measures. I think we would quickly find happiness to be an imperfect metric. How do you define happiness? Is it the same as joy? Or peacefulness? Some people would also push back on the direct link between economics and happiness as relative indicators in the first place.

I would like to see economic indicators that include the percentage of living wage jobs in a community relative to the number of households. Additional indicators are the percentage of jobs with high-quality benefits plans or matching 401(k) contributions. There are also negative indicators, such as degrees of homelessness or the percentage of households paying more than 50 percent of their income toward rent. At the very least, we need indicators that temper the celebratory rhetoric of stock market gains. Many news sites speak of a good economy and the level of the stock market as one-to-one indicators of the economy's health. Homelessness, for example, is considered as an indicator only if it corresponds with increased levels of crime or substance abuse. Still, not having a perfect list of indicators should not preclude us from amending our current system.

In chapter 5, while discussing local strategies, I advocated building relationships with stakeholders and keeping the focus on living wage jobs and the real economy. In a larger context, you can practice skepticism when you hear about a good or bad economy in the media. When you decide which elected officials to support, pay attention to how they define and measure a good economy. Other opportunities to apply this perspective will reveal themselves as we pay attention and keep this in the back of our minds.

Address debt, taxes, and wealth

Uncertainty about what the economy is becoming and whether it is or will be "good" makes us vulnerable to simple narratives about national debt relative to taxes and the US economy's overall health. Worry over the federal debt was popular rhetoric during the rise of the Tea Party in 2010. In 2016, Republicans took control of both houses of Congress and the presidency, and they increased the deficit rather than addressing the debt. To a degree, worry over the debt is a straw man argument to attain power and then ignore the debt issue, but debt is also a legitimate concern. The debt cannot grow forever and becomes more expensive as interest rates increase.

The best way to address the national debt is to cut spending and increase taxes. The problem with cutting spending is that we've already cut spending for many demographics. Significant cuts to spending would likely mean cutting entitlements to seniors, healthcare benefits for children and families (unless we reform the healthcare system itself), benefits for veterans, or further cuts to infrastructure or education.

The only alternative is to raise taxes. In our current system, which has increased wealth inequality, the obvious solution is to raise taxes on the wealthy. There is some hope that tax cuts might lead to increased innovation, which improves the economy and increases the total amount people are paying in taxes. However, we have used this argument for over forty years, and we know it does not work out that way. The wealth generated by tax cuts gives the wealthy more power to advocate for even more tax cuts. If we are authentically concerned about the national debt, we must raise taxes on the wealthy and apply more wisdom to our conversations about federal spending. Whether and to what degree the national debt is a problem is under scrutiny and can be relative based on political leanings. But growing the national debt at our current pace is unsustainable.

Emphasize the role of unions

Unions are an imperfect tool. The history of unions is rife with corruption and challenges.[2] Nevertheless, the proactive coordination of workers has been the best tool by far in America to combat the push to keep the majority impoverished to benefit the wealthy minority. This has always been a fundamental challenge with the structure of the United States. Unions allow for collective action so workers get their fair share relative to shareholders and ensure they have good wages, benefits, and access to the wealth-generating rise in shareholder value. Christians pursuing economic peacemaking and contributing to the national conversation should emphasize the role of unions and support unionization in many sectors.

The Catholic Church has a long history of supporting unions and worker rights. The Poor People's Campaign started under Martin Luther King Jr. and the Southern Christian Leadership Conference, and many churches and Christians support its modern manifestation, which emphasizes access to living wage jobs, in part through increased union membership.

Carefully consider work requirements legislation

Many of us have a pervasive fear of looking foolish or being taken advantage of, at least by certain groups of people. In the United States, that fear drives us to withhold support for struggling households unless we can ensure "they" are not taking advantage of "us." An unintended consequence of this fear is that too many people who do need help cannot get it or cannot get it in a way that helps them stabilize their situation.

Theoretically, the idea that work be an eligibility requirement for federally funded benefits makes some sense. If good jobs are available, we would not want to disincentivize work. If individuals in a community can be earning $30 an hour within thirty or sixty days, right-to-work legislation makes a lot of sense. In that context, there should be a high barrier to justify needing support instead of earning a wage and contributing to tax revenue rather than pulling from it. But in practice, many communities struggle to connect people with jobs that pay more than minimum wage.

Taking a minimum wage job locks you into a hectic life that prevents you from doing other activities like going to school, resting, engaging in community service, or pursuing mental health or substance abuse help. If a job is required to be eligible for a benefit, but the only jobs available pay close to the minimum wage, we are locking people into a system they can't escape. Therefore, economic peacemakers should generally oppose work requirements legislation unless it includes a living wage job stipulation. If it is clear how somebody could earn a living wage, we should try to connect more people with those jobs.

Reform immigration laws

Immigration reform is complicated, controversial, and difficult to grasp fully. One might argue for or against immigration based on a moral stance or the perceived economic benefit or downside of immigrant labor. One person could focus on the affordable housing crisis in the country to argue for greater limits on immigration. At the same time, another could be equally concerned about our desperate need to fill jobs that people currently living here do not want. I would love to transition to an economy that does not depend on undocumented labor to keep costs of goods and services low, but that is our current situation.

As I frequently say in many of my classes, few solutions do not have significant unintended consequences. Often, the proper discussion is not whether this is right or wrong but whether the benefits outweigh the consequences we are unprepared to deal with. If we reduce immigration, we will undoubtedly have less demand for infrastructure. However, since we do not currently have a plan to transition to an economy that functions differently, restricting immigration would result in even fewer workers for entry-level jobs. This would increase the cost of goods and services, and many businesses would shut down because owners could not afford to keep their doors open.

We also need more workers to work and pay taxes for national debt and Social Security obligations. Undocumented workers already pay for these obligations, even though they are ineligible to receive benefits. Many undocumented workers use a fake Social Security number to attain jobs, which means they pay payroll taxes. Others elect to file taxes as an individual tax payer to maintain good standing with the government. This would not mean wholly restricting borders or simply opening them to undocumented workers. Comprehensive immigration reform that allowed more people to come formally so they could work and pay taxes would benefit everyone in our current system.

Consider the merits—and consequences—of universal basic income

Universal basic income (UBI) is a proposed system of providing direct payments to all households in a city or country to ensure everyone has their basic needs provided. There is no defined amount each household would receive or how it would be funded, although taxing large corporations is the default mechanism. There are variations on this theme—guaranteed minimum income, negative income tax, to name just two. UBI has experienced a resurgence in recent years in response to the increased difficulty of finding good jobs alongside inflation. But it has also been an aspirational goal for some. In 1930, the economist John Maynard Keynes predicted his grandchildren would only have to work fifteen hours a week because increases in technology would make each worker so productive we could collectively spend more time on leisure, community, and family.

I wouldn't say I like the idea of universal basic income. When the subject comes up with my students, I call it plan B, but we have to talk about plan B because we do not have a clear plan A. The preferred plan would ensure economic opportunity and all the other social determinants of health with the jobs and resources available in our local communities. If everyone had a clear idea of what the jobs were in their communities that they could realistically attain, and we were connecting them with those jobs, that would be plan A. But what those jobs are is often unclear, and the jobs frequently disappear or do not exist. When jobs do exist, the competencies, degrees, or experience are either vague or unattainable for the people in those communities.

As we've discussed, artificial intelligence will dramatically accelerate these trends in addition to the growing effects of globalization, technology, offshoring, and automation. Suppose large corporations continue to grow by acquiring each other, merging, and using their size and political influence to prevent competition. In that case, the shareholders of those companies will increase in wealth, but the communities affected by these giants will become poorer.

Should we then tax those enormous companies to help mitigate the damage? Suppose a massive retail company enters a community, and all the mom-and-pop and small businesses close because they cannot compete. As a result, that company becomes the town's biggest employer. Then, what if they adopt more automation and technology to eliminate their in-store jobs? How do we help that community? The local economy will struggle to provide jobs because of the ongoing economic gravity of that company. Plan B is a universal basic income. Tax the corporation's profits, along with every other business that has a similar consolidating effect on the economy, and distribute some of that as payments to everyone in the middle class or below a certain income threshold. This is similar to how the state of Alaska shares oil profits equally with every state resident.[3]

The counterargument to universal basic income is that it disincentivizes work. That might be true, but it would also have an unintended benefit. How many more people, if they didn't have to work sixty hours a week doing data entry, would spend time with their families or friends or volunteering, reading to kids at the library, working in their yards, walking around picking up trash, or planting trees? On the other hand, to what degree will necessary jobs in the community go unfilled because people have access to universal basic income and don't want those jobs? It's a hard line to walk, and the United States struggles to walk fine lines as a country right now, which is why I consider a universal basic income plan B.

Ideally, a universal basic income would help pay for the necessities but not for such a high quality of life that it disincentivizes work. If you're struggling to find a job in your community, UBI could afford you a lower-income lifestyle. But you would have to generate additional income if you wanted a car and some disposable income to go to the movies or restaurants. We would probably determine that up to a certain threshold, income from a job adds to the universal basic income. If you pass a certain level of earning, it would start to offset UBI, much like how unemployment benefits work. I'm sure there would be all kinds of unintended consequences to this. Which is another reason universal basic income is plan B. But UBI also has some exciting upsides, which is why it's not plan C.

Support financial regulation

In the late twentieth century, deregulation allowed the US financial industry to run rampant. They created incredibly complex, exploitative financial products, leading to an enormous housing bubble that triggered the Great Recession. In the aftermath of the housing crisis, the 2010 Dodd-Frank legislation provided much-needed regulation. Eight years later, Congress partially repealed the law, raising the threshold of the size of the banks that fell under many of these regulations from $50 billion to $250 billion. Many of the banks that no longer fell under as much scrutiny immediately started engaging in risky behaviors again. In 2023, two banks had to be taken over by the federal government to prevent them shutting down abruptly and sending ripple effects out into the broader economy.[4]

The financial industry will fight to tell us they have learned their lessons and that regulations only hurt their ability to lend money and generate profit and economic activity for the American people. History tells us that the pain of the terrible decisions these institutions make when they are unregulated falls disproportionately on low-income families. Those concerned about economic peacemaking should not believe this argument and should resist further changes to Dodd-Frank.

Pursue comprehensively pro-life policies

The long-term connection between economic peacemaking goals and the welfare and education of children spotlights the overly simplistic pro-life versus pro-choice conversation. Much has been written about the impact of the enhanced child credit from the pandemic stimulus dollars. Direct payments to low and moderate-income parents almost halved the number of children experiencing hunger.[5] It is one of the clearest and best outcomes we have seen.

Ironically, the pro-life contingency largely opposed continuing the enhanced childcare credit, though to their credit, some who initially opposed the expanded tax credit have started to advocate for it after seeing its direct impact on poverty.[6] Those who support the welfare of children, including those in the anti-abortion movement, must comprehensively work to ensure children are thriving after they are born rather than simply ensuring they are born at all. This will become a more significant challenge because of increased restrictions on abortions. These restrictions are likely to lead to an increase in children at risk of adverse childhood experiences. Applying a comprehensive pro-life lens to these conversations rather than simply an anti-abortion lens is critical.

Talk about climate change and the Green New Deal

The Green New Deal has been highly politicized in large part because progressives developed it. It is a proposed set of economic stimulus and climate change mitigation policies. The original resolution was only fourteen pages long and intended to provide a vision for how these goals are complementary rather than competing strategies. The Green New Deal is not perfect, but it is an excellent way to balance economic needs with social and sustainability goals. Climate change is a significant barrier to economic peacemaking and will disrupt many of our current strategies. How do we adapt to a possible housing bubble if the Southwest runs out of water, if parts of the West become unlivable because of constant wildfires, or if coastal regions in the Southeast continue to experience more flooding from rising sea levels?

The Green New Deal is an attempt to talk about shifting the US economy toward sustainability while creating good-paying jobs in emerging sectors. This is an opportunity to resist simple narratives based on political allegiances and engage in more nuanced conversations to understand the best policies to support and advocate.

POLITICAL SYSTEMS

However we define it, a truly healthy economy will mean economic opportunity for many more people. We will not be able to establish an economy that works for most people if we do not have a political system that also represents the majority. Suppose lobbyists and super PACs have disproportionate influence over democratic systems. In that case, there will be no fear of the consequences of increased wealth inequality, at least among those with sufficient wealth to live behind gates that protect them from those consequences.

When I talk about advocacy, policy, and political systems in my community development classes, I can feel the air get sucked out of the room. Everyone gets tense until I assure them this does not mean going on social media and participating in the outrage. In fact, I strongly encourage them not to do that.

Then they exhale, and we talk about civic participation as a cornerstone of a healthy democratic system. This means voting, getting to know the policies of candidates we might support, and communicating with elected representatives about what is important to us. You can write letters to your local and congressional representatives. Elected officials respond to the constituents who vote, advocate, and communicate. Many economic peacemakers are focused on their local communities and dismiss political systems as something for someone else to worry about. Meanwhile, households in the communities we serve keep hitting the same walls and wonder why our systems seem to not be working for them.

The following ideas are not in any way exhaustive or static, but they are a place to start. If democracy does not work for people, the economy will not work for them either. We will all be engaged with political systems to varying degrees, but every economic peacemaker should at least be mindful of political structures and how they can contribute.

End gerrymandering

In the Ken Burns documentary *The Civil War*, historian Shelby Foote claims that "Americans like to think of themselves as uncompromising. But our true genius is for compromise. Our whole government is founded on it." Foote talks about the lack of compromise as a contributing factor that led to the Civil War—a conclusion that not all agree with—but this part of his point is astute: A degree of separation between the states and the federal government, the federal government's three branches, and two major bodies within the legislative branch forces us to compromise to get anything done. The alternatives are to get nothing done—which we've been enduring more of as tribalism makes it risky to collaborate with others—or to throw out democracy and regress to authoritarianism or theocracy.

Compromise is not possible in a gerrymandered system. Gerrymandering is the process of "cracking and packing," cracking the electorate in a given community and packing as many of your political opponents' votes as you can into one district.[7] This leaves your political party with enough votes dispersed among the other districts to maintain political power, even if you have fewer votes. One problem with a gerrymandered system is that moderates who thrive at compromising cannot win seats. In a district guaranteed to vote Republican or Democrat, the more moderate, pragmatic person won't win. The winner tends to be the person furthest to the left or the right. Many Americans appreciate and desire compromise, but the more moderate, pragmatic, empathetic perspective is decreasingly represented.

In 2019, the US Supreme Court elected not to rule on gerrymandering and declared it a states rights issue.[8] Of course, in a state that is gerrymandered, the majority of people who might want to end the practice of gerrymandering do not have the political power to do so, at least without historic turnout. Anyone enthusiastic about economic peacemaking should advocate for and support legislation to outlaw gerrymandering and turn over the creation of districts to independent counsels.

Restore protections on voting rights

In 2013, the US Supreme Court struck down a key provision of the 1965 Voting Rights Act that prevented restrictive voting laws designed to make it difficult for minorities to vote. States immediately started implementing these laws again, including making voter registration more difficult, purging voter rolls, reducing early voting opportunities, closing polling places, changing voter ID requirements, and limiting mail-in voting, among others.[9] If a healthy democracy is critical for a healthy economy, then voting rights are essential to reinforce that democracy. The John R. Lewis Voting Rights Advancement Act, proposed in 2023 and named for the late senator who long fought for civil rights legislation, would go a long way toward restoring some of those protections.

Ultimately, the goal of restoring voting rights is not just preventing a negative outcome but rediscovering a love of democracy. We should aspire to be far more disturbed about the idea of someone we disagree with politically not being able to vote than when they do vote for a candidate or policy we don't support. The idea of anyone being restricted from voting should be abhorrent. We should aspire to be proud to participate in a system in which the candidate we support might lose if they do not appeal to the majority or do not have the best ideas. In a healthy democracy, there is a silver lining when your preferred candidates lose, because it's better to know democracy is working than to ensure your side is amassing the most power.

Promote civic engagement and education

In part because of voter restrictions, voter turnout and participation are frustratingly low in the United States. I used to teach an American culture course for an international exchange program, and the European high school students in my class would always want to focus on the United States' issues with gun violence. As we would get into some of the dynamics of how our systems work and why we're seemingly unable to do anything about it, I would ask the European students what voting was like in their communities. One day, a few students said the turnout in their community was pretty low, with around 75 percent of eligible voters participating. In my city's most recent local election, voter turnout had been 11 percent. They were horrified. In some of the most high-profile recent

US presidential elections, we've exceeded 50 percent turnout, but not by much.

Participation in a democracy is hard because it can feel like any one vote doesn't count. High-quality civics education— telling the story about why participating is just as much about honoring our commitment to this system as it is about affecting the outcome—is a precursor to achieving policy results. If more people voted and participated, we could quickly achieve some of the economic peacemaking outcomes at scale. This would, of course, have to be paired with something like the John R. Lewis Voting Rights Advancement Act to help ensure equal opportunity for political participation.

Christians are already mobilizing and there are excellent faith-based movements doing good work, such as Sojourners, Red Letter Christians, the Christian Community Development Association, and Christians for Social Action. Churches are also historically popular locations to host polling sites.[10] As with anything else, the precise strategies may not be clear when you start. If you care about a topic, I urge you to start listening and building relationships, and the opportunities to move the needle will often present themselves.

Restrict campaign finance spending

The 2010 *Citizens United v. Federal Election Commission* US Supreme Court decision ruled that restrictions on independent political spending violated the First Amendment guarantee of freedom of speech. As described in chapter 3, this removed many restrictions on campaign finance.

Economic peacemakers should support legislation to appropriately limit campaign finance. *Citizens United*, for example, opened the floodgates for super PACs and dark money that funds political campaigns. Many of these resources are used to support candidates, advocate for policies, and promote conspiracies and simple narratives that counteract economic peacemaking efforts.

Engage reparations and land return

The United States owes debts to various communities, and rather than continue to advocate for the merits of colorblindness in a system built on racism that provided generational wealth to some and restricted it from others, we should finally own up to it. I do not know what reparations look like. Would it be direct payments or a long-term investment in housing or education? How would we balance this social justice issue while addressing the peacemaking challenges of providing economic opportunities to struggling communities? Do we not also owe a debt to the coal miners in West Virginia who were so critical for our energy sector and are now seeing their industry decline? This challenging conversation is one well worth having.

The idea of repaying these debts can be overwhelming, but it is gaining traction. In 2021, the city of Evanston, Illinois, became the first American municipality to use a cannabis tax to fund a reparations program with overwhelming community support.[11] Churches and faith groups are finding ways to support historically marginalized neighborhoods in their communities around the country. Others are finding ways to return land or proceeds from land to local Native American tribes.[12] These conversations also lead to public/private partnerships that might not have previously been explored.[13] In Tacoma, for example, the Puyallup Tribe partnered with a regional airline to open a local seaport.[14]

COMMUNITY AND UNITY

Unity is critical for mutual benefit and building space for productive compromise. Christians, in particular, are advised throughout the New Testament to prioritize unity, so in theory, we should be well prepared to lead in building unity. Western countries have always been divided between the wealthy and poor, owners and laborers, conservatives and progressives, White people and people of color, men and women, corporations and unions, rural and urban areas, and so on. The bitter division is part of our heritage, but so is the struggle for more empathy and unity. Peacemaking is much more feasible when we are united behind a common goal, which leads to more unity.

Of course, unity is much like perfection in that we should strive for it with the understanding that it will never be fully achieved or maintained. Unity based on mutual trust and respect allows for disagreement and conflict, creating an opportunity to increase wisdom and find a resolution. In the same way that we do not want false peace that is really just silence, we do not want unity based on conforming to authority. Christians are vulnerable to expecting unity based on not being disagreed with, or on not questioning the "most spiritual" person or person with the most spiritual authority. The apostle Paul calls for unity, and he does not hesitate to admonish Christians.

Focus on allies, but be ready for reconciliation

Since American culture tends toward tribalism and vitriol, economic peacemakers must pursue unity with enthusiasm and realistic expectations. Some people are committed to spite or will not let go of the golden idols that make them feel comfortably in control. I try to be okay with this and to recognize that we're all at different stages of our journeys. That does not give us the license to harm, traumatize, or disrespect others in the meantime, so we will still find ourselves in conflict even as we pursue unity.

However, just because someone might not be open to listening and growing empathy today does not mean they cannot have a change of heart down the road. Some people deny systemic racism until they or their loved ones experience it for themselves. Some people want to get rid of the police until their home gets burglarized. Some wealthy people think the economy is doing well for everyone; therefore, struggling people are at fault for their situations. Then, perhaps they start volunteering with a nonprofit or ministry program and realize how brutal the economy and job market have become for average people.

We need to recognize when someone is not ready for empathy so that we do not compromise our resilience, but we also need to remain committed to being in a relationship with difficult people and actively listening. That also means rejecting any opportunity to say "I told you so." And it means saying "Thank you" as much as possible.

Practice telling and listening to stories

In the United States and elsewhere, much dialogue has devolved into accusations, simple narratives, and defensiveness. We look for "gotcha" and "I told you so" moments everywhere we can, and we work hard to preempt any of those moments being used against us.

But the power of our stories is shockingly underutilized. When someone accuses me of being a socialist and a heretic, that doesn't mean anything or persuade me in any direction. But that same person could tell me a story about themselves that articulates why they believe what they do. Suddenly, I'm their biggest advocate, even if we disagree fundamentally. My most boring conversations are with people I am in total agreement with. Conversations with people who disagree with me but do not talk about their stories or values are dull because there is no honesty or real communication. Far and away, the best and most interesting conversations are with people where there is mutual trust and respect and substantial disagreement. It is an opportunity to sharpen how I talk about things and hear stories and values that might change my perspective.

Most of us are not accustomed to telling stories, especially ones with us in them. But it speaks to the power of storytelling to build unity that even stories told in a clunky and awkward way persuade and endear far more than articulate and techni-cally sound counterarguments. Storytelling is an opportunity to practice healthy disagreement and vulnerability within our churches, within our local communities, and even within our broader social and civic contexts.

Seek reconciliation and relationship between denominations

From a Christian perspective, we see far too much division between denominations, and I believe much of it is related to the ideas explored in this book. We will always have disagree-ments about theology, in large part because we have different cultural lenses and life experiences that influence how we read Scripture or practice religion. Disagreements over sexuality, money, race, justice, and so on are tough, but we should have them with a solid commitment to unity. Christians should be comfortable living with the tension of trying to be morally pure in our behavior, addressing the fact that we often fail to do so, and needing to build relationships with and love our neighbors all at the same time.

I am not advocating for an end to denominations per se. Rather, we should collaborate and communicate when it comes to identifying and advocating for policies that remove obstacles to serving our neighborhoods.

Hone a revival that looks unfamiliar and uncomfortable

There is a lot of hope for a modern revival in Western Christianity. I, too, am hopeful for a Spirit-led resurgence of the church. But are we ready for what that would mean, or would we end up hypocritically squashing the revival because it is not what we were expecting God to do? Many of the religious elite in Jesus' day expected the Messiah to come, overthrow the Roman empire, and install his earthly kingdom. Some of us today have similar expectations for what a revival might produce. But imagine a revival that looks like Acts 2. The new believers praised God and fellowshipped with one another, but they also sold their possessions and sought to meet everyone's needs.

We do not know how a revival might manifest. I must recognize that the behaviors of a revival might not align with my economic peacemaking aspirations, even though I am confident this work results from honoring God's calling in my life. I pray that we can all remain vigilant and adaptable to the unpredictable nature of a genuine revival.

DISCUSSION QUESTIONS

1. What would it mean for your community to be thriving?
2. Which of these policies resonates with you as an opportunity that might affect your community? Which least resonates, or which do you disagree with and why?

3. Think about a familiar context in which there is division where you would like to see a commitment to unity and reconciliation. It might be family, church, work, school, a kids' soccer team, and so on. What do you think are the roots of that division? What might be the first steps to increasing unity in that context?

4. What do you think or hope a revival might look like? What would the impact of that vision have on economic peacemaking goals, if any?

8

RESILIENT PEACEMAKERS

Daring to set boundaries is about having the courage to love yourself, even when we risk disappointing others.
—Brené Brown

A queen does not just run off to play! The queen isn't afraid of a bit of hard work.
—Bluey, in *Bluey*

Peacemaking requires a lot of patience, economic and workforce development can be complex, and community engagement is taxing. Wages for this work are low, especially if you approach it from a ministry context. Meanwhile, the cost of living is high and rising. We have friendships and families, our churches need leaders, community groups need volunteers, nonprofit organizations need board members, and people coming up behind us need mentorship. We also have personal goals and personal needs, and our most precious resource, time, is scarce.

When someone engages in economic peacemaking at any level, much like any ministry or volunteer work, it comes at the expense of something else. Many economic peacemakers get fatigued and burned out before they maximize their potential impact. This work is a long-term effort and, therefore, requires proactive thinking to be a resilient peacemaker who not only endures but thrives.

I'd like to tell two stories about Linda and Simon—syntheses of students and colleagues I've encountered over the years. Linda and Simon represent early-career peacemakers, in part because I tend to work with that demographic, and in part because that is when burnout and fatigue is often likely to occur. Aspiring peacemakers might see some of themselves in these two servants, and church and nonprofit leaders might see some of their staff and leaders as well.

LINDA THE HERETIC

Linda is a former student of mine with a story that mirrors many others. She grew up in a Christian family and regularly attended church. She experienced trauma during her childhood and teen years. Her church community did not handle this perfectly, but they generally supported and loved her. She credits those relationships with helping her find the courage to seek counseling and become a healthy adult. She experienced love and compassion there and felt like she could understand what it meant to love a neighbor as oneself.

Linda has a heart for service and is compassionate, so she decided to attend a Christian university to understand what a career in ministry or related service might be. She earned her undergraduate degree but was unsure what direction her career should take. Maybe she should pursue nursing to have a skill to help people directly or a business degree so she could earn more money and give it away or create jobs for other people. She decided she wanted something with a more robust theological or ministry component. When she enrolled in one of my graduate programs, she was thinking about the traditional international missionary route. But, as for many younger generations, that didn't feel like an appropriate investment. Linda intuited that Christians need to rebuild trust with communities, help meet needs, and empower others, but she could not see what that might look like.

Linda started researching her community to learn about its unmet needs. One data point was particularly alarming. LGBTQIA+ individuals make up somewhere around 5 to 15 percent of the population in her hometown, but nearly 50 percent of youth experiencing homelessness. After learning more about the issue of LGBTQIA+ youth homelessness, Linda decided to make it the central focus of her thesis research.

Linda traveled to Europe to volunteer and do research with a Christian nonprofit that helps transgender youth transition out of trafficking. She heard story after story about men who had entered the trafficking sector out of economic desperation. Once in it, they would quickly find out that they could make more money engaging in transgender prostitution because the demand was higher.

When Linda returned home, she started volunteering for a similar American Christian nonprofit, where she heard story after story of LGBTQIA+ youth being rejected by their Christian families, becoming homeless, and turning to prostitution to make money. The more Linda heard and learned, the more urgently she wanted to intervene and serve. She shared what she had learned with her home church. It seemed clear to her that this was a demographic with whom Jesus would sit down and eat meals, inviting himself into their homes.

She knew that, politically, her church community had strong feelings about gender and sexuality and saw marriage as being between one man and one woman. Like many younger people, Linda did not agree with all these feelings, but she could empathize with her faith community. Still, this was a different situation. No matter one's political or theological stance on gender identity and sexuality, LBGTQIA+ individuals should not be facing such rejection, homelessness, isolation, and trauma. Linda expected her community to respond with compassionate enthusiasm. She wanted to focus on economic peacemaking with this marginalized population, to help them attain jobs to avoid homelessness and prostitution and access other services they might need to heal.

Almost immediately, however, individuals in her church started making accusations. They called her a socialist and a heretic. Satan was deceiving her; she was buying into the lies of the liberal media, and she wasn't reading her Bible. She tried to explain what she had seen, to tell the stories of people she had met. The judgment increased and became more severe. Her own family was frustrated with her for causing so much trouble.

Linda plowed ahead with an economic assessment of her community. To her surprise, the affordable housing and homelessness problem was more widespread than she knew. She had heard the rhetoric about homelessness in the big cities and the choices they must make that led to that outcome, but not in a moderate-sized suburb like hers. There were not as many tent encampments, but they were starting to pop up. She heard about people couch-surfing, parking cars in odd places overnight, eviction notices, talk among renters about tenants' rights, people moving further away, and employers with low-wage jobs unable to find anyone to fill them.

So, there was an acute problem in Linda's community with a vulnerable demographic disproportionately experiencing homelessness and suffering, something she was convinced Jesus would respond to compassionately. Still, she kept encountering anger in her church, where she had expected to find compassion. And not just anger toward the people she wanted to love but anger and bitterness toward Linda for continuing to discuss these issues. One day, Linda again brought up these issues of youth homelessness and who was experiencing it at a church ministry meeting. Afterward, an attendee approached her and said she would be praying for her because Linda had become a child of Satan. That was Linda's last day at church. She started to identify with the growing category of borderline agnostics who "love Jesus but can't stand Christians."

Linda is doing great work in a different community today, but she is not formally part of any church and does not have a way to do her community work in partnership with Christians. Linda hasn't given up yet, but many former Christians have been pushed into doubt or outright atheism because they did not embark on their economic peacemaking journeys sufficiently prepared to encounter hypocrisy or idol worship within the church.

SIMON THE GOOD AND FAITHFUL (AND TIRED) SERVANT

Simon grew up in a rural community and, being a pragmatist, stayed home and completed a two-year degree online at a regional community college to save money and avoid debt. He could not find a job in his local community that would pay him to work with youth or to address an issue he cared about, such as trafficking. So he moved to a bigger city in the same state to pursue a job in the social services sector.

In the city, homelessness and other signs of distress were notably more visible, but there were also more organizations working to meet those need. Simon heard a lot of rhetoric around solving problems, which he was hungry for. He applied for as many jobs as possible, focusing on nonprofits or church positions concentrated on ministry. He was eventually invited to interview for a case manager position at an organization that provided services for women and children who had survived domestic violence and also operated a substantial food pantry. The interview went well, and he was offered a job paying $45,000 per year. In his home community, that would have seemed like a lot for an entry-level job, but Simon quickly discovered that did not go very far in the city. Unable to find an apartment he could afford, he rented a room from someone who needed a roommate.

The website for this nonprofit looked fantastic. There were photos of classrooms full of people learning about jobs and graduates in hard hats working in what were probably living wage jobs. He was assigned to a grant and told he must reapply to receive this grant again. The grant was not related to anything on the website. The initiative raised awareness about EBT (food stamps) in the low-income community. Many people qualify for food stamps or Medicare but are not enrolled, sometimes because they are unaware they are eligible. This grant seemed unrelated to the organization's mission, but the communications manager told Simon it was necessary because it allocated 10 percent of the total grant funding for general administration. This was intended to cover the cost of administering the grant, but the organization depended on piecing together as many grants like this as possible to pay for the leadership team, who would then focus on the core mission. It seemed a little convoluted, but Simon was a team player, so he wrote the grant application. He was also asked to help with the organization's social media presence and to work on writing and posting materials.

A few weeks later, Simon was instructed to look for other grants that could substitute for the food stamps initiative if it were not awarded again. Simon was under the impression that since the initiative was not related to the mission and vision of the organization, they would not pursue a new funding source if that grant ended. But the communication manager told him the executive director wanted to, so they must find a way to keep it going.

Three years later, Simon's responsibilities at the organization had grown. He was now a manager and was earning $3,000 more per year than when he first started. His monthly rent had also increased by $300. Simon was still working on grants, and although the number of grants he was responsible for had grown, none were related to the initiatives listed on the website. But he was still told that they supported the mission.

The executive director called him into his office about once a month to put pressure on him to find more grants. The organization had grown and expanded its scope, but it did not have clear data about its work or the outcomes it had achieved over the years. More donors and funders started noticing and were more reluctant to give money. Simon had taken over events coordination and was responsible for the annual fundraiser, during which the executive director would get up in front of a room of donors and local elected officials and give a lengthy speech about his passion for the mission and why the work they did was so important.

Meanwhile, Simon's income barely covered his necessities. He worked fifty to sixty hours a week for the nonprofit and sometimes worked side gigs on the weekends. He told himself all this work was for the mission of the organization. He thought a lot about the youth and those engaged with trafficking. He had started out passionate about serving, so he kept going. Since moving to the city, Simon had not attended church or read his Bible. He still considered himself a Christian and prayed silently when he walked down the street, but that was about the extent of his spiritual engagement.

One day, Simon's roommate told him he would be moving to another city for a new job. Simon started apartment hunting and was alarmed to find that other rooms for rent were significantly more expensive than his current rent. He went to the executive director and told him he would be transitioning out by the end of the year because he needed to find a new job. The executive director was flustered, muttered something about loyalty and service, and dismissed Simon. Simon went home and started looking for his next job.

A few days later, the organization's deputy director asked to meet with him. The deputy director was a long-suffering servant in the community who had outlasted three executive directors. She understood Simon's situation and acknowledged the tight budget, but she did not want to lose Simon. Several other employees had left within the past year because they could not afford to stay in the community at the organization's wages. The deputy director offered Simon a new role that consolidated the three vacant positions into a director role. This new position would be stressful, but the pay would be $65,000 a year. Simon was thrilled to accept.

Five years later, Simon had relentlessly been doing the work of three people. He was earning $70,000 a year. His small apartment ate up almost half of his take-home pay. The executive director had left, as had the deputy director. Many staff positions were frequently unfilled or were filled by interns or AmeriCorps student staff members. One day, Simon attended a senior leadership meeting. The city's community services department had not been impressed with the last few years' progress reports. The grant writer position had experienced high turnover, and the newest grant application to the city to renew funds had been scored relatively low. The organization would be excluded from any city funding for the next biennium. The new executive director explained that the organization could not keep its doors open. Another nonprofit organization that ran a domestic violence shelter would assume the operations of the domestic violence programs. The future of the food bank was unclear. Layoff notices would go out at the beginning of the following month.

During a visit home shortly thereafter, Simon met a high school friend for coffee. He heard about his peers getting married, buying homes, and starting families. Simon suddenly realized how tired he felt. He worked so much that he did not have time for exercise. He didn't have opportunities or disposable income to socialize. He'd been on some dates over the years but was not in a relationship, even though that was something he wanted. He did not make enough money to save for a down payment on a home. He didn't really have time to develop other skills or hobbies. There had been a time when he felt sorry for his peers because his work felt so purposeful, but now Simon felt disillusioned.

In the nonprofit sector or other ministry work, Simon's experience is not uncommon. For some engaged in ministry work, sometimes this results in switching sectors. Sometimes it leads to an effort to enhance skills to be more entrepreneurial and intentional in managing one's career in economic peacemaking. Simon ended up in my program, where we emphasize the latter.

BUILDING RESILIENCE

As a community economic development teacher, I have always understood that part of my job is to equip students with the competencies they will need to endure and succeed, even if they cannot yet see why and when they will need those skills. This ability to be resilient and endure without sacrificing health and life goals has always been a priority but I did not often articulate it, even though I have embedded it in all my courses.

Even before the COVID-19 pandemic, but especially during and since, I started seeing students entering the program already burned out and fatigued. It's not everyone, but it's certainly more prevalent. I have had to pivot and enhance the part of the programs that emphasize learning how to rest and heal despite the high volume of work.

Often, one's twenties are spent grinding to cultivate skills, experience, and a reputation that launches workers' careers in their thirties and forties, which allows them more time and financial flexibility to find balance. But doing this work within a ministry or nonprofit organization can sometimes lock workers in a grind that never ends or pays off. Then those workers turn forty-five and realize they have put off their life goals in pursuit of a mission. Sometimes, they made substantial progress toward that mission, and sometimes, they discovered part of life passed them by and they didn't have the impact that was worth the sacrifice. So a critical question is, How can economic peacemakers impact the world and not only endure but thrive, whether this work means a career in a nonprofit or finding ways to volunteer or lead in one's local community?

ENGAGING IN REST AND SELF-CARE
Rest and sleep
The nonprofit and ministry worlds are not immune to the cultural celebration of unhealthy work habits. We love to come to work and talk about how tired we are, how little sleep we get, and how hard we work. It's hypocritical to call this out

because I'm a chronic overworker with too many projects. But I have at least learned to stop celebrating it.

The best boss I ever had pulled me into her office one day after I had sent an email at ten o'clock the night prior. As people frequently do, I had been checking my work email at night and responded to an email. It was essential, and I wanted to be perceived as timely and reliable. My boss told me she was not impressed by my sending an email at ten at night; in fact, she was disappointed. I should prioritize spending time with my family and sleeping. I learned my lesson, and now I advise my students to stop participating in this race to be the least healthy and instead celebrate how much rest and exercise we are getting.

Physical health

Physical health is not something we often talk about in careers and service. Each new year, we might prioritize health and identify goals for that year. But many of our systems exploit the energy and enthusiasm of youth to get by. Organizations often assume that you should be making sacrifices if you're in a helping position. That includes your time, your financial health, and your physical health. So we celebrate not sleeping, we talk about how little time we have for extra exercise, and we may snack as a coping mechanism. Our bodies are more resilient when we are young and can overcome some of this.

In the long run, we are cultivating habits that are hard to break. This is rarely a malicious act by organizations trying to operate on shoestring budgets; it is just an unhealthy habit and value we have developed due to not talking about it. Proper nutrition, exercise, and work-life balance are critical for effective and long-term economic peacemaking.

Mental health

There was a time when I was running multiple community meetings every month during the school year. I appreciate the importance of having routine meetings so people build a habit of attending. But I also try to value people's time, so even though I worked to make each meeting meaningful and productive, occasionally we did not have a clear purpose to meet. Whenever that happened, I would send out a cancellation notice with a specific instruction: Rather than using this time to get caught up on other work, please use this time to take a mental health walk.

When I switched from running to swimming, I was surprised to encounter silence. Normally I would listen to an audiobook on my headphones or bring a tablet to the treadmill so I could work while exercising. But Bluetooth does not work in water, so when I swim it's an hour of silent exercise. This added feature has had a tremendous effect on my mental health. I didn't realize how much media and technology were affecting my mind and spirit.

Social media promises more connections and more opportunities to experience diversity. In practice, it becomes just the opposite. When I was in the Peace Corps, it became an excellent way to share photos and updates with family and friends. But in many ways, it has become antisocial media focused on maximizing profit. Social media is terrible for our mental health, for our perceptions of how well other people are living, and for consuming false information and outrage. Undisciplined time on social media only immerses us in ideas from people who think pretty much like us or bots and artificial intelligence that pretend to think like us, rather than engaging us with a more diverse perspective that leads to empathy.

We need more exposure to opportunities to discover what we do not know rather than having simple narratives affirmed. I advise my students to have a strict rule of staying off social media or having strict guidelines for using it. It can be an effective tool, but if we perceive what's happening in the world or get our news diet only through social media, we must assume we are misinformed. We are undoubtedly overlooking opportunities for empathy, curiosity, context, and nuance.

THINKING STRATEGICALLY

Economic peacemaking can be hard work, but sheer effort and number of hours is not always what is called for. Many aspiring leaders have burned themselves out being too busy, sometimes doing things that do not lead to outcomes in the community. To cultivate resilience, we need to consider not just how much we can do, but precisely where we invest our limited time, energy, and attention.[1]

Resist simple narratives

We must be automatically skeptical of simple black-and-white narratives. Depending on their attitude, when someone tells me that all homelessness is a result of choosing drugs over responsible behavior, I usually end the conversation. Some people prefer to do drugs, and that can lead to homelessness. Even in those cases we need to be sympathetic to genetic dispositions to addiction or life circumstances such as being prescribed opioids by a physician. But for many people substance abuse is a result of becoming homeless due to the loss of a job, mental health issues, or a lack of affordable housing options, and substances never come into play.

Still, someone who staunchly defends a black-and-white narrative will not be convinced otherwise. So when I hear overly simplistic narratives rigorously defended, I kick the dust off my sandals and move on to the next person or situation. Our theological, political, and economic contexts are complex, nuanced, and intertwined. Resilience can be undermined by fighting simple narratives that will not be undone by head-to-head conflict.

A feeling of scarcity, or not having enough, can make us more vulnerable to these simple narratives. In the community economic development world we talk a lot about scarcity mindsets. Maybe you are stressed about finances, not getting enough sleep, do not feel safe, have health issues, do not have loving relationships in your life, do not feel like people respect what you have to say, have too much on your plate, or are concerned with the well-being of a family member. In fact, almost everyone experiences scarcity at any given time that undermines our resilience, but we have a cultural stigma against acknowledging it.

Imagine for a moment that someone whom you respect comes up to you, puts their hand on your shoulder, looks into your eyes, and says, "You are doing well, and everything is going to be okay for you and your loved ones." How would your mind, let alone your physical body, respond to that, assuming you believe that person? I imagine a feeling of sudden decompression, because we all have tension from worry that love, safety, and dignity are scarce and fragile.

As a parent of three children, I experienced quite a few years of not getting enough sleep, working too much because we were a single-income family, and feeling the pressure of financial scarcity since I primarily work in the nonprofit sector. My capacity for taking in context, for holding my tongue when I'm offended and giving others the benefit of the doubt, for flexing that muscle of curiosity and empathy, goes out the window when I am tired and fatigued. I have believed simple narratives that were presented during periods of scarcity mindset, and I have been blessed to have enough of them shattered from subsequent life experiences. So this becomes a compounding strategy. Purging simple narratives builds resilience, and resilient people are resistant to simple narratives and have the emotional and mental capacity to think in more nuanced ways.

Ask where you fear the "I told you so"

Being resilient also means being a hopeful and curious person. Spite and outrage displace curiosity and empathy. So to be resilient economic peacemakers, we need to be aware of our vulnerabilities and tendencies toward bitterness.

One way to look for these vulnerabilities is to consider where we are anxious that someone might tell us "I told you so," or where we are eager to declare that to someone else. The most obvious example is politics. We all know someone we think is wrong about their political perspectives or information. It would, in theory, feel so good to prove them unequivocally incorrect and tell them, "See?! I told you so! This person was evil, or this person was not pure evil. Or this person was amazing, after all!"

But fearing another's "I told you so" can make us unwilling to try anything at all. We pass up opportunities to try out new things or perspectives. And if you have ever had the chance to deliver a devastating takedown to someone else, you probably realized it is worth almost nothing. The desire can be all-consuming, but the act does not satisfy the desire at all. This is how spite and bitterness double down on each other. Like greed, they are never satisfied. The more we start down the road of greed, resentment, or spite, the more we desire greater depths of greed, anger, and spite. We respond to opportunities to be more spiteful or outraged. Therefore, it can be helpful to ask, Whom do I desire to prove wrong? Whom do I despise or feel bitterness toward? Realizing the absurdity of this dynamic and repenting for it moves us back toward hopefulness and curiosity, which are exceedingly resilient.

Beware the search for villains

Related to the idea of simple narratives is the hunt for the villains responsible for all our woes. That takes up a lot of our attention and time. If something is wrong in the world, it is because a bad guy must be found and defeated. In the anti-trafficking world, there is frustration over the obsession in media and movies with sex trafficking as essentially only kidnapping and exploitation. An evil person kidnaps a young girl, then she must be rescued through violent intervention. We might imagine Liam Neeson's character in *Taken* vengefully hunting down the bad guys one by one to get his daughter back.

Sometimes kidnapping is the case, but much trafficking results from economics and includes not just sex trafficking but labor trafficking as well. Children work in terrible conditions and youth enter prostitution as a result of not having economic opportunities in their communities. But the narrative that there is a bad guy at the heart of any problem also means the solution is to defeat the bad guy. It is easier to think about sending a hero to save someone from trafficking than to wonder about the ethics of buying a product assembled by children or enjoying a service that is affordable because workers are not paid a living wage.[2]

The current global rise of nationalism and populism are examples of people taking advantage of fatigue and scarcity mindsets to push simple narratives about villains who must be defeated at all costs. Some of the more significant events of the twentieth century were genocides and wars based on simple narratives in hard times about villains responsible for complex societal woes. In the same way we need to work out our muscles of curiosity, empathy, and resisting simple narratives, we should develop skepticism over blame-game talk.

I will practice this myself here. I often call out corporations and billionaires as problems. Too much wealth is concentrating at the top. Certainly, there are wealthy individuals and organizations doing harm intentionally, but I generally do not see these stakeholders as villains. They are humans and human-made organizations responding to incentives. If a system provides an opportunity to hire a lobbyist to advocate for policies that increase your wealth, you will probably do so. In the same way that the pursuit of unity does not preclude conflict, some wealthy stakeholders will fight back against possible changes. That does not excuse demonizing all wealthy people or assuming that every wealthy person intends to exploit others.[3]

The constant search for villains and the relentless finger-pointing are exhausting efforts that take capacity away from peacemakers. Knowing we are all part of systems that exploit for profit whenever they can get away with it and trying the best we can moving forward preserves our ability to keep learning and acting.

Don't let the perfect be the enemy of the good

Economic peacemaking requires understanding that the world is increasingly globalized, complex, and interconnected. There are few right or wrong answers, and even with clear solutions, there are always unintended consequences. But we should not let perfection be the enemy of the good, especially since very few issues have clear solutions with no downside. Crime will

increase if we do not provide sufficient jobs and economic
opportunities. If we hire more police to deal with that crime,
we will put more people in jail. But jails and prisons famously
do not prevent future crime. People who go to prison are traumatized and might get connected to gangs. When they come
out, they have a tough time finding a decent job or career
pathway, so they might give up and return to criminal activity.

Accepting the world's complexity, which is more gray than
black-and-white, leads to a genuine grieving process, but on
the other end is more resilience. Some Christians who get into
economic peacemaking start out intending to be like twen-
tieth-century missionaries who raised financial support from
American churches to live overseas. But then they learn the
history of how missions was entangled with colonialism and
capitalism, and they start to see more people in their local
communities unable to meet basic needs. After a grieving
process, some of them leave Christianity; they can't find a
community that resonates with them. Still others might commit to working through their local churches to meet needs and
advocate for families.

In my graduate program, the first semester provides a lot of
context regarding psychology, culture, and what is happening
in communities and the economy. That first semester provokes
something akin to a grieving process for many students. The
world is more complex and nuanced than they often realized.
But then, for the rest of the program, this grieving process
enables them to dig into the context of their local communities
and uncover opportunities to serve and make an impact that
they were previously unaware of.

Acknowledging these complexities is not easy, especially
when we know there are "I told you sos" around the corner
for good but not perfect interventions, but doing so is essential

for fostering resilience and addressing root causes of economic and social challenges. Embracing nuanced understanding can lead to more compassionate, effective policies that reflect the interconnectedness of our global community.

Challenge the fear of failure and the allure of celebrity

Cultivating resilience is as much about establishing boundaries as lowering them in strategic places. We spend a lot of time avoiding competencies that can lead to success and pursuing ones that lead to nothing. If you are interested in developing a superpower, build up a resistance to the fear of failure and short-term embarrassment. If you want to make mental and emotional space to put that power to good use, cleanse yourself of the cultural lust for status and celebrity that has preoccupied and distracted many would-be economic peacemakers.

Many of us spend so much time thinking about ourselves: how we look, what others are thinking about us, the last thing we said, what we're going to eat, our money or status. But we often have far less capacity to care about random people for very long. So while you might remember times of embarrassment with horror, chances are nobody else remembers or cares. Yet we often exert so much effort to avoid embarrassment. In his classic joke about the disproportionate power of this fear, comedian Jerry Seinfeld notes that the number-one fear is public speaking, followed by the fear of death. So if you're at a funeral, he quips, it's apparently better to be in the casket than giving the eulogy. When we embrace the reality that embarrassment is like cotton candy—it dissolves so fast it barely registers for others—there can be a brief moment of grieving when we realize other people aren't particularly concerned with us. Friends and family are, but most others aren't. But that sense of loss can quickly be replaced by relief. Released of the anxiety of embarrassment, we are increasingly able to take risks in pursuit of something worthwhile.

If embarrassment is like cotton candy, failure is like eating broccoli. It may not be pleasant to eat (at least before you acquire a taste for it), but it is good for you. Failure not only shapes our character for good or ill depending on how we react to it, but it also influences how much others come to trust us. If we get defensive when we fail, we can appear insecure and are often trusted less. If we fight to avoid failure or hesitate to do good work until the strategies are perfectly clear and victory is assured, we can look immature or selfish. When we take a chance in good faith, relying on data and relationships as best we can, failure can sometimes be a good or at least acceptable result. When we own up to a failure, take responsibility for it, and learn from it, trust and respect often skyrocket. Economic peacemaking is complex, controversial, and difficult. Failure is inevitable, so we might as well make it work for us and let it become an investment in long-term success.

Much like broccoli when you get used to eating it, you can develop a taste for embracing failure. You can learn to appreciate its benefits. Then you look around and realize you've adopted behaviors that employers and partners are looking for, and you're asked to take on more responsibility. It's a superpower any of us can develop, but most of us shy away from it. Yes, there is a difference between failure in pursuit of something worthwhile and failure as a result of incompetence or poor execution, so it is always important to discern your motives.

If shedding the fear of embarrassment and failure is like developing a superpower, a desire for status and celebrity is our kryptonite. Western culture is obsessed with attaining these goals. Many aspiring economic peacemakers push to attain minor (or major) celebrity status, theoretically to grow their influence and maximize their systemic impact. In reality, these ambitions are like any other idol—they eventually become the goal in and of themselves. Where an organization needs to focus on doing one thing well, a misguided executive director might push it to grow in order to cultivate personal influence and progress a political career. We might start a campaign to tell a story that grows empathy, only to find ourselves obsessed with going viral or cultivating a large following. After a while, we can lose our sense of empathy and turn to maximizing wealth and followers.

I believe that the aspiration of anyone doing ministry should be to serve in anonymity. It is part of our calling. Jesus warned believers not to practice righteousness in front of others to be seen (Matthew 6:1), and he celebrated those who clothe others in need or visit people in prison (25:36). Paul warned believers against selfish ambition and vain conceit (Philippians 2:3).

The more we flex our superpower and avoid our kryptonite, the more we will behave in confident and humble ways. Ironically, this can lead to accusations of self-righteousness and vain conceit—which only calls for more humility. Only you can scrutinize your motives, but demonstrating confidence with humility can be a sign of growing in maturity as a resilient economic peacemaker.

Learn to say no

Part of being a young person starting out in any career is saying yes to too many things. You must make as many investments in your network, skills, and reputation as possible to establish your career pathway over time. After a while, you realize your time and attention are your most precious resources. How you invest and manage your limited time and attention defines who you are and your impact on the world.

Even today I struggle knowing when and how to set boundaries and say no. One of the challenges with navigating a career pathway or life of service in economic peacemaking is encountering lucrative opportunities that offer financial security but would take you away from the frontline work. You might love case management or working directly with youth, but those opportunities are often volunteer positions, or they pay closer to the minimum wage. Higher-paying positions are more administrative and closer to leadership than direct service. So, on the one hand, as your career develops, you will be inclined to continue to volunteer or take on contract jobs to continue to invest time and attention in the community. On the other hand, if you balance that with a family, social life, and other obligations or goals, you risk burnout. There is no perfect strategy, but each person must think proactively about their limited time and how to balance priorities.

Articulate life goals

Westerners are pressured to be consumers, but earning enough money to consume or to pay off the debt accumulated by consumption can displace other life goals. As a ministry-minded financial coach, I have a lot of conversations with people where we uncover the realization that their goal is to attain enough money, somehow, to have both disposable income and disposable time. Even wealthy people often feel they have to work so much they do not have disposable time, and people with leisure time rarely feel they have enough financial resources to not worry about money. That is only a problem if we give in to the pressure to be passive consumers or to try to achieve goals other people have for us.

If we do the work to understand what we value and what our goals are, then the strategies that balance time and money start to emerge. Some people say they just want a life of video games and travel. As a financial coach, I don't judge. I appreciate the honesty and clarity. We then work out the math for how to maintain that lifestyle with the minimum number of working hours not spent playing or traveling. I also have leisure goals, but I wanted a life of service and a more traditional family life and house. That is a monumental goal in our expensive modern society. The ability to attain a graduate degree, get married, have a family, buy a home, and do so while earning relatively little money in the nonprofit sector requires clarifying goals and investing time and attention to attain them.

CULTIVATING COMMUNITY

One of the joys of teaching for a community development program is building a community for people who feel alone in their values and the work they are trying to do. I am accustomed to hearing the phrase "I thought I was the only one." But many Christians believe we needed to think about jobs and policies with empathy and curiosity and seek to follow through on the commitment to love God and love our neighbors as ourselves.

In addition to the practical side, many people are inclined to distrust Christians because of traumatic experiences they have had with or in churches. So many young Christians are eager to repent to the broader community for previous generations of Christian behavior and then do the work of reconciliation and build more peaceful communities. But like Linda the heretic, they find opposition in many of their church communities. There is resistance to the idea that Christians ever did anything wrong. And therefore, there is no need to repent.

This dynamic has pushed many young Christians away from the faith entirely. A large percentage of young adults in my graduate program are deconstructing their faith. They still love Jesus but are hesitant to become involved with churches or other Christians again—all the more reason that I'm thankful they are in our faith-based program and haven't given up on us yet. So the program, in addition to equipping for community development best practices, is also a place of healing and rest for weary sojourners. By the program's second year, they're often in a different and more confident place. Ready to return to the world more equipped with new insights and tools to have an impact when it comes time to work on their thesis, papers, or projects.

Some of my students' initial ideas often include convincing the other people in the church that they were wrong and need to repent and do better ministry. Sometimes that is the right project for somebody. Still, I often counsel students to think about going in a different direction. If we perceive greed and Christian participation in wealth and an emphasis on the size of the stock market as not just a mistake but a slow walk toward idolatry, that problem cannot be fixed with a white paper or a five-point plan.

Some people are gifted prophets who are sent or empowered to work with Christians who have fallen into idolatry and probably do not even realize that is what they are experiencing. But most of the time, my students do not feel compelled to prophesy. They feel compelled to serve and to love their neighbors. What they want is to repent, reconcile, and build peaceful communities. And that will not be accomplished by convincing people to walk a different path. That will primarily be achieved by building coalitions of people who also see that this work needs to be done well and who also thought they were alone or a part of a much smaller community than is the case.

Have realistic expectations for the community you serve

For those involved in any social service or peacemaking work, realistic expectations for the behavior we encounter in the community are critical for maintaining resilience for the duration of a career. Nonprofit workers are known for often being naive and adopting a "nobility of the poor" mentality. We sometimes believe systems are evil while people are generally good. If you remove the constraints of the cruel system, people will then make good choices. More people certainly would make good choices given economic opportunity and solid home situations growing up. But trauma and hopelessness certainly are not erased by removing obstacles in the short term when somebody is already a young adult or adult.

We also need realistic aspirations for the communities we serve. When I lived overseas, I ran a young adult science club in my neighborhood. Two young men would come by the club and make fun of us regularly. After about six months, they occasionally would come inside and participate. I did not realize that they wanted to participate but were too embarrassed. By the time I moved, those two had taken on leadership roles and were raising money from local businesses to expand and sustain the club. I should have had higher aspirations and been on the lookout for leaders in disguise.

I recently asked one of the men from our dads' initiative what he's learning from the community he works with. What stands out most to him, he said, is how much community members want to help but don't know how. But whenever there is an opportunity for authentic conversation or a meaningful project, community members support it enthusiastically. When opportunities are restricted it is easy to assume a lack of care or concern when the opposite is usually true.

On the rare occasion that we feel like we have sufficient resources and strategies to help communities in need, when we identify an accelerated training program with employers eager to hire, we might have people in the community enthusiastically sign up and then drop out of the program because they don't want to engage activities that might preclude their employment. Perhaps they express sincere anxiety about being able to support their children, but they like drinking alcohol, and they would have to drive for the job we are training for, so they refuse. Sometimes people learn the technical skills required for a job but struggle with the soft skills an employer prioritizes. Sometimes people show up chronically late or disappear. Other times, people work hard, finish their program, and enter new jobs. Peacemakers are vulnerable to early fatigue and burnout when they do not see the frustrating failures coming. Because they do. Some people will continue to make bad choices that hurt themselves and their children regardless of the opportunities provided to them.

We see others using that frustrating behavior to justify not trying to help anybody, so I understand why we fight to see the good in every opportunity. But to be resilient and do this work over the long term, we have to know how much help we can extend to each person and not spend too much time on those not yet ready to advance. This is also how economic peacemaking is a complementary, collaborative process. Someone stable and prepared to get trained for a living wage job should have people fully invested in helping them achieve that goal. Someone else may not be ready yet, and rather than giving up on that person, we need others to provide compassionate care, relationships, access to healthcare, and so on, with realistic expectations.

I can get burned out when I encounter the needs of people who are not yet ready to engage tools I have to offer—helping connect folks with training and living wage jobs. I stop thinking about living wage jobs and systems to train people for them. Others get burned out trying to think about jobs and want to create safe spaces for people to rest and heal before they have to jump back on the hamster wheel. Both of us need to know our strengths and to lean into those with excellence, and both of us would fail without the other.

Focus on collaboration over conflict

A consistent theme in this book has been avoiding fruitless conflict and focusing instead on coalition building. Some people love to fight and thrive on arguments and conflict. I have learned to love productive conflict. Some of my closer relationships are with people who disagree with me strongly, but we both trust we are arguing our perspectives in good faith. Even though our conversations can get heated, there is always a mutual curiosity because we know there are good reasons that person thinks differently. We want to learn from that perspective.

Conflict both online and in person is often not like this. People frequently argue in bad faith, look for "gotcha" moments, and do not hear you when you are talking because they are just thinking of the next thing to say that might rattle you. That is not a good use of time and energy. Jesus tells his disciples, "If anyone will not welcome you or listen to your words, leave that home or town and shake the dust off your feet" (Matthew 10:14). The apostle Paul went to Athens and saw the city full of idols, so he preached to the philosophers who just wanted to talk but never acted. Some of them followed him, but many of the philosophers just sneered, so he moved on (Acts 17:16–43).

Some of us will be called to ministry to the embittered, but that will require a commitment to long-term relationships of love and mutual respect. It will look much more like Jesus refusing to stone the woman caught in adultery than hurling accusations at people who are closed off to us emotionally because they sense we do not like or respect them. And this is good news, because fruitless arguments are exhausting. Finding other people also committed to making peace so that we can scale our efforts is much more exciting.

Be together as a church community

One of the joys of teaching graduate programs is learning from international students from all over the world as they share their perspectives on community issues and how to address them. It is always a stark reminder of how individualistic Western cultures are, and we sometimes forget the value of community in pursuit of individual goals. When you talk to people who grew up Christian but now consider themselves agnostics or atheists, they often tell you they miss the community they used to get from church.

Being part of a community is a critical aspect of resilience. In Paul's letter to the Galatians, he instructs them to "carry each other's burdens, and in this way you will fulfill the law of Christ" (6:2). When the author of the book of Hebrews calls for Jesus-followers to persevere, he adds, "Let us consider how we may spur one another on toward love and good deeds, not giving up meeting together, as some are in the habit of doing, but encouraging one another" (10:24–25).

I read as many books as I can about faith-based community development, economic development, and peacemaking. Many saints are doing excellent and innovative work in their communities in response to the issues discussed throughout this book. But there is one theme I have noticed frequently enough that I make little notes whenever I encounter it. There is often some variation of "getting people back in the pews." That feels a little like an individualistic appeal. Churches that work together to make peace and pursue unity end up building strong communities that grow. A small church in my neighborhood has a simple motto: "Pick up a shovel." They do just that, and work to meet their neighbors' needs. The church is growing—and their numbers include some people who had almost given up on church altogether.

DISCUSSION QUESTIONS

1. What is a cultural expectation or value that might be undermining your resilience?
2. What is at least one mindset or habit you could cultivate to enhance your resilience?
3. What are your three to five primary life goals or values?
4. If you were to engage in the work of economic peacemaking, which might potentially compromise your resilience?

GREATER THINGS

Very truly I tell you, whoever believes in me will do the works I have been doing, and they will do even greater things than these, because I am going to the Father. And I will do whatever you ask in my name, so that the Father may be glorified in the Son. You may ask me for anything in my name, and I will do it.

—John 14:12-14

Inconceivable!

—Vizzini, in *The Princess Bride*

Jesus, the guy who told Peter to get the money they needed to pay their taxes from a fish he would catch, commanded the storm to subside, turned a little bit of fish and bread into more than enough to feed a crowd, healed the sick, gave sight to the blind, and raised a dude from the dead, said whoever believes in him will do even *greater* things? Why do I care so much about living wage jobs? Let's just distribute fishing poles to get the money we need to pay rent, live off fish and bread, and turn water into wine. That sounds great.

That is somewhat tongue-in-cheek, but as I continue to grind and struggle to do my part to make peace in my corner

of the world by enhancing economic opportunity for historically marginalized communities, these words are often on
my mind. Many books have been written, and sermons have
been preached on this passage. Is it literally for us right now?
Is it for the apostles who would go on to perform miracles
themselves? Is it about the cumulative work of the church
over generations?

I don't fret about precisely what Jesus did mean, but I do
think about what he didn't mean. Because Jesus also said to
consider the birds of the air and the lilies of the field—"they
neither sow nor reap nor gather into barns; yet your heavenly
Father feeds them; . . . they neither toil nor spin." If God feeds
the birds and clothes the grass, how much more will God care
for you, says Jesus. "Therefore do not worry, saying, 'What
shall we eat?' or 'What shall we drink?' or 'What shall we
wear?' . . . Your heavenly Father knows that you need all these
things. But seek first the kingdom of God and His righteousness, and all these things shall be added to you. Therefore do
not worry about tomorrow" (Matthew 6:26–34 NKJV).

This is yet another opportunity to be shrewd as a serpent
and innocent as a dove, by both having faith that God will provide for his people and being prudent with our resources and
energy to help one another. One of the most aspirational parts
of the Bible for our modern times is Acts 2. The result of being
filled with the Holy Spirit and asking the apostles, "What shall
we do?" was both worship and meeting each other's needs. Of
course it was. The natural result of being excited about God
and praising him is wanting to love your neighbor. Praising
God when people in need surround you would be unnatural
and make no sense. If a dam breaks, the water will flow out.
But meeting needs without praising, fellowship, prayer, and
joy inhibits the Lord from adding to our numbers.

ECONOMIC PEACEMAKING *AS* CHRISTIANS OR *BECAUSE* WE'RE CHRISTIANS?

Part of my responsibilities while serving in the Peace Corps included directing a national youth entrepreneurship initiative, which required raising funds from Dominican businesses and individuals to support aspiring entrepreneurs. When I returned to the United States, I started working for a regional workforce development council. They appreciated the work that I had been doing and the money I was raising, and they wanted me to replicate it. I explained that the fundraising was actually the last piece of the puzzle. It started with relationship building, understanding context and needs, testing some ideas, scaling up the ideas that worked, and then looking for partners to elevate and sustain the projects.

The initial stages of that workforce job were difficult. This was 2013, and we felt like we were still recovering from the Great Recession. During the recession, nearly a trillion dollars of stimulus money had been poured into the system to identify and retrain laid-off workers. Much of that money had been spent on building administrative capacity to handle cumbersome federal and state contracts, which ballooned some organizations. Finally, jobs were starting to be more plentiful, and there was a lot of work to be done, especially in historically marginalized communities, which had been recovering much slower. But organizations also knew they would have to reduce their workforces as stimulus funds dwindled, thus the eagerness to find money elsewhere.

I explained to the leadership team that we did not need to replace the millions of dollars in dwindling federal funds because it looked like we could solve many of the problems we were facing with the partners we already had. We needed to collaborate and line everyone up to function as a pipeline of services, from low-income communities to living wage jobs, winding through support services and training programs. I told them I would create a pilot project to show them what I meant.

I partnered with a local technical college, maritime employers from the port, and the school district to build a ten-week certificate program for credit-deficient high school seniors. That summer, eighteen students completed the inaugural program and were offered interviews or the opportunity to apply to matriculate into a maritime program at another technical college. I had advocated that if this worked, we should replicate this relationship-based dynamic with employers from other sectors. Right before the inaugural program started, I was laid off. The leaders who had been skeptical and antagonistic to the idea then took credit for the initiative and used it for their election campaigns.

It was not as dramatic as it might sound, but it did force me to stop and think. I had attended Bible college where I trained to be a missionary, then transitioned to holistic ministry in a desire to love my neighbor, which led me to economic peacemaking. But there are few mechanisms to do economic peacemaking as a Christian, so I started working for nonprofit and public organizations. I was happy to do this work while also volunteering and serving in my local church community. But I had just experienced the limitations of what I could do. The Calvary cavalry did not arrive to support me in replicating my good ministry work.

At that time, I started wondering how I might do this work *as* a Christian and not just *because* I am Christian. It is not uncommon for Christians to spend their weeks seeing homeless encampments, witnessing children who are growing up in scarcity, and so on, then go to church on Sundays looking for an individual spiritual experience. It's hard to know how to live, love, and serve as a Christian, partly because we have other responsibilities and partly because we often do not know what to do.

My first doctorate is in ministry, specifically semiotics, or the study of signs and symbols. How do we learn to read the signs of what God is doing in the world, the story God is telling in our communities, and what our roles might be? Shortly after I helped develop that maritime program, my teaching career began, in addition to running more complex economic peacemaking projects. As my economic peacemaking work has taken shape, more of my capacity is becoming dedicated to equipping other individuals and communities to enhance their ministry and service with an economic peacemaking lens. We can do greater things together.

IDEAS FOR SOME GREATER THINGS

The fascinating dynamic about honoring this promise for greater things is it might take us in many unexpected directions. Perhaps we will be led away entirely from direct economic peacemaking as a goal and find something else we were not expecting. Some might implement radical visions for an empathetic economic peacemaking initiative in our communities. Perhaps you might feel called to run for office yourself and commit to doing so with the understanding that the position is an opportunity to serve, not a throne to be won. Some churches or coalitions of faith-based communities might establish and manage mobile home parks or other housing options. As lower-middle-class housing options have dried up, mobile homes and parks remain relatively affordable, albeit scarce. Building more lower-cost housing options and managing them with integrity is a tremendous opportunity to meet a need and love our neighbors.

Churches could support local cooperative businesses or housing developments. Many entrepreneurial types of work, such as cleaning services, thrive more quickly if they work together under one business name. They can share marketing efforts and other resources while maintaining client bases and managing income streams. Many communities have interest in cooperative housing that essentially functions as transitional housing. But in a cooperative model, you have a financial stake in a unit and accumulate equity as you live there, make payments, and contribute to the community. When you leave, you recoup that equity, allowing you to invest in housing or some other goal you are working toward.

One example of this kind of co-op housing is a limited equity cooperative. In this model, homes are only allowed to be sold to low- and moderate-income households. This creates opportunity for more families to enter the housing market, although it limits the equity one can earn in the home because of resale restrictions. Churches sometimes partner with community development corporations, or start their own, to develop cooperative housing. One of the oldest cooperative housing models is based out of Seattle and was started in the 1940s.[1] Some churches, such as Peace Presbyterian in Eugene, Oregon, have converted part of their land into affordable housing, especially as congregation sizes have dwindled and their land has become more valuable.[2] There are numerous instances of Black churches converting fellowship halls and land into housing solutions that both address the affordability issue and provide additional income to support the churches.[3]

Faith-based communities can participate in community land trusts and purchase land with a long-term vision for a city or region's sustainability or economic peacemaking goal. We can provide the tools, training, and space for urban farms and vertical farms to provide employment, leisure activities, and access to healthy food for more households in dense urban areas. We can facilitate and build more art programs for youth. We can then help youth in those art programs understand that they are learning the competencies required for living-wage jobs. We can help transition young adults from a youth art program into a job training program they find themselves more prepared for than anticipated. We could help establish childcare centers for working parents or encourage employers to establish their own childcare centers and help manage them. We could advocate for and help run grocery stores in areas that would otherwise be food deserts. There are many outlandish ideas, all of which are opportunities for generosity, empathy, innovation, creative problem-solving, collaboration, and risk-taking.

WHO IS YOUR NINEVEH?

In the story of Jonah and the whale, we tend to focus on Jonah's being swallowed by the whale for three days. We remember that he was not doing what God asked, admitted he was at fault when the storm came, and volunteered to be thrown overboard to save the ship and crew. That part of the story is so strange that we tend to overlook the beginning of the story and why he was running from God in the first place. Jonah was a prophet, a man of God. And God called him to the people Jonah did not want to be saved. He did not run away from God because he was scared, he ran away because he did not like God's plan.

One consistent theme in the Bible is how God subverts our expectations. God picks the youngest of the brothers, David, to become the king of Israel. God tells Jonah to go to the place he least wants to go. The coming king did not establish an earthly kingdom but a spiritual one. The king who was supposed to rule died on the cross. The people he ate with and spent time with were not royalty or the religious elite but the tax collectors, prostitutes, and other sinners.

I must be disciplined to remember that the economic peacemaking work enhances and complements our other ministry and community service activities. But what is the bigger picture? What is the broader story God is telling? What, if any, is my small role in that?

Even as I ask those questions, I am mindful that the health, wealth, and prosperity gospel has crept into my thinking and theology in ways I still do not fully understand and that I'm still rooting out. When I think of the greater things God may call us to, in addition to or in place of economic peacemaking, it might be grander and more exciting. It also might be a call to preach to the Ninevites. So, who is my Ninevah? Whom do I detest and dislike? What would my response be if God called me to serve them, either with direct economic peacemaking or by pursuing some other, unpredictable ministry?

WISE AND FAITHFUL SERVANTS

I did not start out intending to be an economic peacemaker. My goal was to do holistic ministry, building relationships with the community to understand what they need and meet those needs in service to the commitment to love my neighbor as myself. Ironically, if I had started with the intent to build an economic peacemaking career, I imagine I would have had less success. I may have gotten slotted into a more traditional economic development role and stayed there. Perhaps that would have been ideal. But to the degree that my career has been worthwhile, it has resulted from holding it with an open hand and trying to understand the story God is telling in the

community and what my small part in that story is. So far
that has meant hearing what is happening in the community
and authentically and transparently responding to those needs
with passion, empathy, and respect. I'm still committed to
hearing and obeying with an open hand. Perhaps my career
will deviate into something other than economic peacemaking, or maybe that will continue to grow.

In working to equip peacemakers, my aims are not to have
more people draw a circle around economic peacemaking and
commit to that as a career pathway. I hope that we grow in our
empathy and curiosity, understand more context, and assume
there is something more interesting and nuanced than the simple narratives and simplistic solutions often presented to us.
Empathy and curiosity may lead us to something akin to economic peacemaking, workforce development, grassroots community development, education, mental health counseling, and
so on. It might lead to more people working in nursing, sales,
and car maintenance who continue their careers with excellence and grow in empathy and curiosity—finding innovative
ways to contribute their skills and stories to the community.

Economic peacemaking may be our calling and our expres-
sion of loving our neighbor as ourselves, but in the end the
value of the jobs themselves will not amount to much. Jesus
paints the bigger picture for us in Matthew 24 when he muses
with his disciples about the destruction of the temple and
signs of the times. Despite our efforts to make peace, Jesus
says, "nation will rise against nation, and kingdom against
kingdom" (v. 7). His instruction is not to double down on the
peacemaking, but to "watch out that no one deceives you"
(v. 4). Further, he says that believers will be hated by all nations
because of him, and many believers will turn away from their
faith and will betray and hate each other. That will make

us vulnerable to idols and false prophets (vv. 10–11). "Who then," Jesus asks, "is the faithful and wise servant, whom the master has put in charge of the servants in his household to give them their food at the proper time?" (v. 45)

We might be tempted to become economic peacemakers to try to save the world. But it has already been saved. In Romans 8, Paul writes, "I consider that our present sufferings are not worth comparing with the glory that will be revealed in us" (v. 18). Creation, he says, is groaning as in the pains of childbirth, including believers who groan inwardly waiting for the redemption of our bodies (vv. 22–23). "For in this hope we were saved" (v. 24).

We are not trying to save the world. We are trying to love God and love our neighbors, trying to ensure they can live with the dignity of being made in the image of God.

Blessed are the peacemakers.

DISCUSSION QUESTIONS

1. What is God doing in your community?
2. What do you think your part is in that story?
3. How will you continue to pay attention and listen?

NOTES

FOREWORD

1. Shailly Gupta Barnes, Lindsay Koshgarian, and Ashik Siddique, ed., Poor People's Moral Budget: Everybody Has the Right to Live (Poor People's Campaign, 2019).

CHAPTER 1

1. Michelle Alexander, *The New Jim Crow: Mass Incarceration in the Age of Colorblindness*, rev. ed. (New York: The New Press, 2012), 8.

2. "Truck Driver Retention: Stats and Strategies You Need to Know," Drivewyze, last modified December 13, 2023, https://drivewyze.com/blog/truck-drivers/truck-driver-retention-stats-and-strategies-you-need-to-know/#.

3. See, e.g., Vera Yakupova and Anna Suarez, "Parental Burnout, Depression and Emotional Development of the Preschoolers," *Frontiers in Psychology* 14, no. 1207569 (June 20, 2023), https://www.ncbi.nlm.nih.gov/pmc/articles/PMC10318402/.

4. If we were to do this well and at scale, we would run into the challenge of realizing there are simply not enough living wage jobs for enough people to afford a middle-class quality of life. This informs the discussion of state and federal policies for peacemaking described in chapter 7.

5. See, e.g., Conrad Wilson and John Ryan, "FBI Warns of Neo-Nazi Plots as Attacks on Northwest Power Grid Spike," Oregon Public Broadcasting, January 19, 2023, https://www.opb.org/article/2023/01/19/surge-in-oregon-washington-substation-attacks-as-fbi-warns-neo-nazi-plots/.

6. "Make Me Smart," *Marketplace*, November 16, 2021, https://www.marketplace.org/wp-content/uploads/2021/11/Make-Me-Smart-November-16-2021-transcript.pdf

7. Recommendations for further reading include Jemar Tisby, *The Color of Compromise: The Truth about the American Church's Complicity in Racism*; James H. Cone, *The Cross and the Lynching Tree*; Michelle Alexander, *The New Jim Crow: Mass Incarceration in the Age of Colorblindness*; and James Baldwin, *The Fire Next Time*.

8. Jack Ewing, "United States Is the Richest Country in the World, and It Has the Biggest Wealth Gap," *New York* Times, September 23, 2020, https://www.nytimes.com/2020/09/23/business/united-states-is-the-richest-country-in-the-world-and-it-has-the-biggest-wealth-gap.html.

9. This might include alternatives to a traditional job such as entrepreneurship, which is discussed in subsequent chapters.

CHAPTER 2

1. "Rent Market Trends in Tacoma, WA," *Rent*, accessed April 15, 2024, https://www
.rent.com/washington/tacoma-apartments/rent-trends.

2. See, e.g., Andre M. Perry, Hannah Stephens, and Manann Donoghoe, "Black Wealth
Is Increasing, but So Is the Racial Wealth Gap," *Brookings*, January 9, 2024, https://
www.brookings.edu/articles/black-wealth-is-increasing-but-so-is-the-racial-wealth
-gap/.

3. "Financial Opportunity Center Network," *LISC*, https://www.lisc.org/our-initiatives
/financial-stability/financial-opportunity-center-network/.

4. Gregg Robb, "U.S. Household Wealth Rises to Record $154.28 Trillion in Second
Quarter," *MarketWatch*, September 8, 2023, https://www.marketwatch.com/story/u-s
-household-wealth-rises-to-record-154-28-trillion-in-second-quarter-ef85ac85.

5. Centers for Disease Control and Prevention, "Adverse Childhood Experiences (ACEs):
Preventing Early Trauma to Improve Adult Health," last modified August 23, 2021,
https://www.cdc.gov/vitalsigns/aces/index.html.

6. Thomas Insel, "America's Mental Health Crisis," Pew, December 8, 2023, https://
www.pewtrusts.org/en/trend/archive/fall-2023/americas-mental-health-crisis.

7. United Way of Northern New Jersey, "About Us: Meet Alice," United for Alice, https://
www.unitedforalice.org/meet-alice.

8. See, e.g., "Homelessness and Substance Abuse," National Coalition for the Homeless,
last modified September 22, 2020, https://nationalhomeless.org/wp-content/uploads
/2017/06/Substance-Abuse-and-Homelessness.pdf.

CHAPTER 3

1. Bulls and bears often symbolize the stock market or investors—a bull market is
marked by optimism about rising prices and investments; a bear market the opposite.
The iconic *Charging Bull* bronze sculpture erected at Bowling Green in downtown
Manhattan has become a de facto symbol of Wall Street.

2. "The Buffett Indicator expresses the value of the US stock market in terms of the
size of the US economy. . . . Given that the stock market value represents the present
value of expected *future* economic activity, and that GDP is a measure of most recent
actual economic activity, the ratio of these two data series represents expected
future returns relative to current performance. . . . It stands to reason that this
ratio would remain relatively stable over time, increasing slowly as new technology
creates more efficient returns from labor and capital. . . . If the stock market value
is growing much faster than the actual economy, then it may be in a bubble."
"Buffet Indicator," Current Market Valuation, accessed April 18, 2024, https://www
.currentmarketvaluation.com/models/buffett-indicator.php.

3. Matt Philips, "The Rich Now Own a Record Share of Stocks," *Axios*, January 10,
2024, https://www.axios.com/2024/01/10/wealthy-own-record-share-stock-market;
Jack Caporal, "How Many Americans Own Stock? About 158 Million—but the
Wealthiest 1% Own More Than Half," *Motley Fool*, last modified November 1, 2023,
https://www.fool.com/research/how-many-americans-own-stock/.

4. See, e.g., Ana Hernández Kent and Lowell R. Ricketts, "Real Estate Helped Drive
Wealth Gains during the Pandemic," Federal Reserve Bank of St. Louis, August 8,
2023, https://www.stlouisfed.org/on-the-economy/2023/aug/real-estate-wealth-gains
-pandemic.

5. Anne Marie Knott, "Why The Tax Cuts And Jobs Act (TCJA) Led To Buybacks Rather Than Investment," *Forbes*, February 21, 2019, https://www.forbes.com/sites /annemarieknott/2019/02/21/why-the-tax-cuts-and-jobs-act-tcja-led-to-buybacks -rather-than-investment/.

6. Drew DeSilver, "For Most U.S. Workers, Real Wages Have Barely Budged in Decades," Pew Research Center, August 7, 2018, https://www.pewresearch.org/short-reads /2018/08/07/for-most-us-workers-real-wages-have-barely-budged-for-decades/.

7. Irinia Ivanova, "'Greedflation' Caused More Than Half of Last Year's Inflation Surge, Study Finds, as Corporate Profits Remain at All-Time Highs," *Fortune*, January 20, 2024, https://fortune.com/2024/01/20/inflation-greedflation-consumer-price-index -producer-price-index-corporate-profit/.

8. Juhohn Lee, "Why American Wages Haven't Grown Despite Increases in Productivity," CNBC, last modified July 18, 2022, https://www.cnbc.com/2022/07/19/heres-how -labor-dynamism-affects-wage-growth-in-america.html.

9. Elise Gould and Katherine DeCourcy, "Low-Wage Workers Have Seen Historically Fast Real Wage Growth in the Pandemic Business Cycle," Economic Policy Institute, March 23, 2023, https://www.epi.org/publication/swa-wages-2022/.

10. Taylor Giorno, "Federal Lobbying Spending Reaches $4.1 Billion in 2022—the Highest Since 2010," *Open Secrets*, January 26, 2023, https://www.opensecrets.org /news/2023/01/federal-lobbying-spending-reaches-4-1-billion-in-2022-the-highest -since-2010.

11. Economic Policy Institute, "Unions Help Reduce Disparities and Strengthen Our Democracy," EPI, April 23, 2021, https://www.epi.org/publication/unions-help-reduce -disparities-and-strengthen-our-democracy/.

12. For more context, I strongly recommend Erik Loomis's *A History of America in Ten Strikes* (New York: The New Press, 2018).

13. Tim Lau, "*Citizens United* Explained," Brennan Center for Justice, December 19, 2019, https://www.brennancenter.org/our-work/research-reports/citizens-united -explained.

14. Yuval Rosenberg and Michael Rainey, "US Debt Races Toward Record This Decade, CBO Warns," *New York Times*, March 20, 2024, https://www.nytimes.com/2024/03 /20/us/politics/debt-taxes-budget.html.

15. The Affordable Care Act, passed in 2010, focused on providing health insurance rather than reforming the healthcare industry, in large part because of the role of the healthcare lobby. The original ambition of the Obama administration was to include a public healthcare option, which would allow the government to offer healthcare directly and negotiate prices. The legislation was at risk of filibuster. So it was revised to focus on tax penalties for people who did not have insurance (incentivizing healthy and younger people to get it and decrease the cost of insurance for everyone) and expanding Medicare to states to supplement insurance plans for lower income households. Therefore, Medicare spending has increased. The logical solution to reducing this spending would be to revisit a public option and fix the healthcare system. The alternative would be remove the Affordable Care Act and reduce Medicare spending, but that would result in many households losing access to healthcare.

16. National Institute on Retirement Security, "New Report: 40% of Older Americans Rely Solely on Social Security for Retirement Income," NIRS Online, January 13, 2020, https://www.nirsonline.org/2020/01/new-report-40-of-older-americans-rely-solely-on-social-security-for-retirement-income/.

17. E. Napoletano, "Here's How Many Billionaires and Millionaires Live in the U.S.," *Forbes*, last modified October 23, 2023, https://www.forbes.com/advisor/retirement/how-many-billionaires-and-millionaires-live-in-the-u-s/; Americans for Tax Fairness, "Number of Billionaires in the United States from 1990 to 2020," *Statista*, March 7, 2012, https://www.statista.com/statistics/220093/number-of-billionaires-in-the-united-states/.

18. James B. Steele, "How Four Decades of Tax Cuts Fueled Inequality," Public Integrity, November 29, 2022, https://publicintegrity.org/inequality-poverty-opportunity/taxes/unequal-burden/how-four-decades-of-tax-cuts-fueled-inequality/.

CHAPTER 4

1. See Kathryn J. Edin and H. Luke Shaefer, *$2.00 A Day: Living on Almost Nothing in America* (New York: Houghton Mifflin Harcourt, 2015).

2. On child labor and cell phone production, see, e.g., Siddhartha Kara, "Is Your Phone Tainted by the Misery of the 35,000 Children in Congo's Mines?," *The Guardian*, October 12, 2018, https://www.theguardian.com/global-development/2018/oct/12/phone-misery-children-congo-cobalt-mines-drc.

3. Ariel Van Cleave and Will James, "Remembering the Day Tacoma's 'Japantown' Disappeared," KNKX, May 17, 2017, https://www.knkx.org/news/2017-05-17/remembering-the-day-tacomas-japantown-disappeared.

4. Tacoma Pierce County Health Department, "Confronting Anti-Asian Racism (AAPI Equity)," TPCHD, last modified January 15, 2024, https://tpchd.org/i-want-to/learn-about/aapi-equity/; Natalie Saby, "'It's Almost Too Relevant': Tacoma Mob's 1885 Removal of Chinese Immigrants Resonates Today," K5, May 31, 2021, https://www.king5.com/article/news/community/facing-race/tacoma-1885-chinese-immigrant-removal/281-da47e652-fc0e-4aba-ba03-ae8ef533226f.

CHAPTER 5

1. The Workforce Innovation and Opportunity Act was passed in 2014 and replaced the 1998 Workforce Investment Act (WIA) as the primary federal legislation to offer career services and other support for the labor market.

2. To look up a Workforce Innovation and Opportunity Act organization in your region, check out the CareerOneStop Service Locator at https://www.careeronestop.org/LocalHelp/service-locator.aspx.

3. Will James, "A Developer Forced Them Out of Their Building. Three Years Later, Nearly Half Are Dead," KNKX, December 8, 2021, https://www.knkx.org/south-sound/2021-12-08/a-developer-forced-them-out-of-their-building-three-years-later-nearly-half-are-dead.

CHAPTER 6

1. See, e.g., "Creating Community in Digital Gatherings," PCUSA, March 27, 2020, https://www.presbyterianmission.org/resource/creating-community-in-digital-gatherings/.

2. Universal basic income, or UBI, is a social welfare proposal that would grant citizens a regular minimum income. As I discuss in chapter 7, which explores broader policies for peacemaking, I refer to UBI as a plan B strategy because it has significant limitations—but still has some promises.

3. See, e.g., Bernard Marr, *Future Skills: The 20 Skills and Competencies Everyone Needs to Succeed in a Digital World* (Hoboken: Wiley, 2022).

CHAPTER 7

1. See Kathey Hinson, ed., "Why Employers Check Credit and What They See," Nerd Wallet, February 9, 2024, https://www.nerdwallet.com/article/finance/credit-score -employer-checking.

2. See, e.g., John Hutchinson, *The Imperfect Union: A History of Corruption in American Trade Unions* (New York: Dutton, 1970); Erik Loomis, *A History of America in Ten Strikes* (New York: The New Press, 2018); Neal E. Boudette, "United Auto Workers Seek to Shed a Legacy of Corruption," *New York Times*, July 31, 2022, https://www .nytimes.com/2022/07/31/business/uaw-autoworkers-union-corruption.html.

3. The Alaska Permanent Fund is funded by oil and mining revenues, which are paid to state residents to benefit current and future generations of Alaskans. Residents currently receive about $1,600 annually. See Department of Revenue, "Permanent Fund Dividend," PFD, https://pfd.alaska.gov/Division-Info/about-us.

4. David Enrich, "Back-to-Back Bank Collapses Came after Deregulatory Push," *New York Times*, March 13, 2023, https://www.nytimes.com/2023/03/13/business/signature -silicon-valley-bank-dodd-frank-regulation.html.

5. Elise Gould, "Child Tax Credit Expansions Were Instrumental in Reducing Poverty Rates to Historic Lows in 2021," Economic Policy Institute, September 22, 2022, https://www.epi.org/blog/child-tax-credit-expansions-were-instrumental-in-reducing -poverty-to-historic-lows-in-2021/.

6. Rachel M. Cohen, "Inside the Fight for an End-of-Year Deal on the Child Tax Credit," *Vox*, December 5, 2022, https://www.vox.com/policy-and-politics/2022/12/5 /23489576/congress-child-tax-credit-omnibus-tax-lame-duck; Alyssa Rosenberg, "I'm Pro-Choice, but I'm Grateful for What Pro-Life Groups Did This Week," *Washington Post*, February 1, 2024, https://www.washingtonpost.com/opinions/2024/02/01/child -tax-credit-abortion-rights-bipartisan-family-policy/.

7. Nick Corasaniti, Reid J. Epstein, Taylor Johnston, Rebecca Lieberman, and Eden Weingart, "Redistricting Explained: Your Questions Answered," *New York Times*, November 7, 2021, https://www.nytimes.com/interactive/2021/11/07/us/politics /redistricting-maps-explained.html.

8. Yuri Rudensky and Annie Lo, "Supreme Court Refuses to Stop Partisan Gerrymandering," Brennan Center, June 27, 2019, https://www.brennancenter.org /our-work/analysis-opinion/supreme-court-refuses-stop-partisan-gerrymandering.

9. Jasleen Singh and Sara Carter, "States Have Added Nearly 100 Restrictive Laws Since SCOTUS Gutted the Voting Rights Act 10 Years Ago," Brennan Center, June 23, 2023, https://www.brennancenter.org/our-work/analysis-opinion/states-have-added-nearly -100-restrictive-laws-scotus-gutted-voting-rights.

10. Daniel Silliman and Jared Boggess, "20% of Polling Places Are in Churches. We Mapped Them," *Christianity Today*, October 3, 2022, https://www.christianitytoday .com/ct/2022/october/church-polling-place-election-democracy.html.

11. Associated Press, "Evanston, Illinois, Becomes First U.S. City to Pay Reparations to Black Residents," NBC News, March 23, 2012, https://www.nbcnews.com/news/us-news/evanston-illinois-becomes-first-u-s-city-pay-reparations-blacks-n1261791.

12. See, e.g., "Kansas Woman Donates Part of Farm Sale Profits Back to Tribe," AP News, last modified February 11, 2019, https://apnews.com/general-news-7f2d5d907fc8431280245e5e6195b3.

13. See, e.g., Michelle Cyca, "Vancouver's New Mega-Development Is Big, Ambitious and Undeniably Indigenous," *Macleans*, March 11, 2024, https://macleans.ca/society/sen%cc%93a%e1%b8%80%b5w-vancouver/.

14. Bellamy Pailthrop, "Puyallup Tribe's Partnership with Kenmore Air Takes Off with Scenic South Sound Seaplane Flights," KNKX, August 11, 2023, https://www.knkx.org/south-sound/2023-08-11/puyallup-tribe-kenmore-air-tacoma-south-sound-seaplane-flights.

CHAPTER 8

1. For more perspective about servant-hearted work as play, I recommend Leonard Sweet's *The Well-Played Life: Why Pleasing God Doesn't Have to Be Such Hard Work* (Carol Stream, IL: Tyndale, 2014).

2. For more examples of how our hunt for a villain to blame usually ends with realizing it's us, I strongly recommend Hans Rosling, *Factfulness: Ten Reasons We're Wrong About the World—and Why Things Are Better Than You Think* (New York: Flatiron Books, 2018).

3. For more on considering this dynamic, see, e.g., Henri J. M. Nouwen, *A Spirituality of Fundraising* (Nashville: Upper Room Books, 2011).

CHAPTER 9

1. "Capitol Hill Urban Cohousing in Seattle—An Overview," Capital Hill Urban Cohousing, last modified March 18, 2023, https://capitolhillurbancohousing.org/overview/.

2. Andrew Heben and Jeffry Albanese, "Why Combining Community Land Trusts and Limited-Equity Cooperatives Benefits Residents," *Shelterforce*, April 5, 2024, https://shelterforce.org/2024/04/05/why-combining-community-land-trusts-and-limited-equity-cooperatives-benefits-residents/.

3. Naida Mian, "Black Congregations Are Developing Housing on Church Land," *Shelterforce*, January 17, 2023, https://shelterforce.org/2023/01/17/black-churches-become-affordable-housing-developers.

THE AUTHOR

Brian Humphreys is a community economic development professional who is passionate about enhancing local churches' capacity to love their neighbors. He first trained to be a missionary pilot, but soon became aware of the growing struggle for households to attain living-wage jobs. He is both an academic and a practitioner, executing projects in the community while training the next generation of Christian leaders and servants. Brian cares deeply about the intersection of Christian peacemaking and the global challenge of economic inequality. He is an assistant professor at Northwest University in Kirkland, Washington, and has served as the director and chair of the School of Global Studies, where he designed and launched a master's program in community economic development.